General editor: Graham Handley

Brodie's Notes on Charles 1
David Copperfield

Graham Handley MA PhD
Formerly Principal Lecturer in English, College of All Saints, Tottenham

Pan Books London and Sydney

First published 1987 by Pan Books Ltd,
Cavaye Place, London SW10 9PG
9 8 7 6 5 4 3 2 1
© Pan Books Ltd 1987
ISBN 0 330 50254 9
Photoset by Rowland Phototypesetting Ltd, Bury St Edmunds, Suffolk
Printed and bound in Great Britain by
Richard Clay Ltd, Bungay, Suffolk

This book is sold subject to the condition that it
shall not, by way of trade or otherwise, be lent, re-sold,
hired out or otherwise circulated without the publisher's prior
consent in any form of binding or cover other than that in which
it is published and without a similar condition including this
condition being imposed on the subsequent purchaser

Contents

Preface by the general editor 5

The author and his work 6

Plot and background 9

Chapter summaries, critical commentaries, textual notes and revision questions 13

Dickens's art in *David Copperfield*
The characters 80
David Copperfield 81, Mr Micawber 87, Mrs Micawber 88, Uriah Heep 89, Betsey Trotwood 91, Mr Dick 92, Steerforth 93, Traddles 95, Dora 96, Agnes 97, Other characters 98

Style 104

General Questions and Further reading 111

References in these notes are to the Pan Classics edition of *David Copperfield* but as each chapter is analysed separately, the Notes may be used with any edition of the book.

Preface

The intention throughout this study aid is to stimulate and guide, to encourage the reader's *involvement* in the text, to develop disciplined critical responses and a sure understanding of the main details.

Brodie's Notes provide a summary of the plot of the play or novel followed by act, scene or chapter summaries, each of which will have an accompanying critical commentary designed to emphasize the most important literary and factual details. Poems, stories or non-fiction texts will combine brief summary with critical commentary on either individual aspects or sequences of the genre being considered. Textual notes will be explanatory or critical (sometimes both), defining what is difficult or obscure on the one hand, or stressing points of character, style, plot or the technical aspects of poetry on the other. Revision questions will be set at appropriate points to test the student's careful application to the text of the prescribed book.

The second section of each of these study aids will consist of a critical examination of the author's art. This will cover such major elements as characterization, style, structure, setting, theme(s) for example in novels, plays or stories; in poetry it will deal with the types of poem, rhyme, rhythm, free verse for example, or in non-fiction with the main literary concerns of the work. The editor may choose to examine any aspect of the book being studied which he or she considers to be important. The paramount aim is to send the student back to the text. Each study aid will include a series of general questions which require detailed knowledge of the set book: the first of these questions will have notes by the editor of what *might* be included in a written answer. A short list of books considered useful as background reading for the student will be provided at the end.

The General Certificate of Secondary Education in Literature

These study aids are suitable for candidates taking the new GCSE examinations in English Literature since they provide detailed preparation for examinations in that subject as well as presenting critical ideas and commentary of major use to candidates preparing their coursework files. These aids provide a basic, individual and imaginative response to the appreciation of literature. They stimulate disciplined habits of reading, and they will assist the responsive student to analyse and to write about the texts with discrimination and insight.

Graham Handley

The author and his work

The biographies and critical studies of Charles Dickens – and they show no signs of abating – are testimony to the powerful hold he has exerted on the reading public ever since the first appearance of *Sketches by Boz* (1833–4). In the eyes of many he stands next to Shakespeare; television plays and scripts are written about his life or aspects of it, and his books are filmed, adapted, or turned into musicals (Lionel Bart's *Oliver!*, for example), with flattering regularity and ingenuity. The biography, *Charles Dickens*, by his friend and adviser John Forster, tantalizes both by what it reveals and what it omits; while F. R. Leavis, perhaps the most influential critic of the novel in the twentieth century, has recanted his view (expressed in *The Great Tradition*, 1948) that Dickens was merely 'a great entertainer'.

This study aid can do no more than give the outlines of a crowded life, both creative and social, direct the student to the experience of a great writer, and perhaps to some of the critical and biographical works which will help to extend his own experience of the books. Childhood exercised a peculiar influence on Dickens, perhaps because he felt that his own was scarred, and the student of *David Copperfield* should read those other novels which explore the trials and tribulations of childhood: *Oliver Twist*, *Hard Times* and *Great Expectations*.

Born in 1812 in Portsmouth, the second eldest son in a family of eight, Dickens saw his improvident father and the rest of the family incarcerated for debt in the Marshalsea Debtors' Prison. This experience was to receive full treatment in *Little Dorrit* (1855–7): Charles spent six weeks working in Warren's blacking warehouse before his father's release and his own despatch to school. Again he was haunted by what he had endured, and part of the autobiographical element of *David Copperfield* records the anguish of the time. Dickens lived as he wrote, with zest and with an unrivalled capacity for experiencing both the ecstasy and the melancholy and later incorporating these extremes into his fiction. He worked in an attorney's office; then as a reporter in Doctors' Commons, teaching himself shorthand and quickly striking out as a writer himself under the pseudonym of 'Boz'. The first sketches referred to above were followed by the episodic *Pickwick Papers* (1836–7), which were originally commissioned as a vehicle for the artist Seymour; their verve and humour, their presentation of a range of eccentric and idiosyncratic characters, and the animated and ebullient style and control of situation, established the young author who, before he had finished them, became editor of *Bentley's Miscellany*, and began to write *Oliver Twist*, the first instalment appearing in the magazine in February 1837.

In May 1837 his sister-in-law Mary Hogarth died; she had lived with her sister and Charles since their marriage, and Dickens adored her. She died in his arms; he took a ring from her finger, and wore it until his own death. He dreamed of her continually, and there is little doubt that many of the heroines of his fiction are derived from the purity and perfection he found in her.

Oliver Twist was followed by *Nicholas Nickleby* (1838–9), an attack on the Yorkshire farm schools. Dickens was never less than prolific, and *The Old Curiosity Shop* (1840), *Barnaby Rudge* (1841) and *Martin Chuzzlewit* (1843–4) indicate his capacity for giving himself wholeheartedly to the career he had already made so successfully for himself. Active socially, theatrically, politically, philanthropically (his letters reveal the amazing range of his interests and concerns), he spent longer from now on than hitherto between his novels. But increasingly a growing sense of artistic structure came upon him, and from *Dombey and Son* (1846–8) that awareness is present in the complex handling of plot and sub-plot, of contrast and parallel, of image and symbol. Of course it leads to the creation of long and bulky novels (which Henry James referred to as 'loose, baggy monsters'), and these perhaps deter the modern reader from total immersion in Dickens. They occupy the middle section of Dickens's career, with *David Copperfield* (1848–50), perhaps the best-loved, and *Bleak House* (1852–3), the most aesthetically pleasing. Between that and the prison-riddled *Little Dorrit* (1855–7), Dickens sandwiched a small masterpiece, *Hard Times* (1854), set in the (for him) distant provincial location of Preston (Coketown). He had spent much of his time in Paris, and a reading of Carlyle's *French Revolution* is said to have kindled a desire to write *A Tale of Two Cities* (1859), with its graphic reconstruction of events great and small in that turbulent era. But strictly speaking the last period of Dickens's writing begins with *Great Expectations* (1860–61), thought by some critics to be the high watermark of his achievement. It is rich in the experiences of childhood and in atmosphere and, as in *Our Mutual Friend* (1864–5), there is no evidence of any falling off, either in the verve or the vivacity of the writing or of the imagination that informed it. The final work, *Edwin Drood* (1870), which seemed to be breaking new ground, was left incomplete by the author's death.

Then there were his stories (remember, for example, that ever-popular allegory, *A Christmas Carol*, 1843), the playlets, essays and speeches.

No mention has been made here of Dickens's private life, save the reference to Mary Hogarth's death, and his devotion to her. A description of the separation from his wife and his relationship with Ellen Ternan is, we feel, irrelevant to these study notes. Like most writers, Dickens is surrounded by anecdote and gossip, by interpretations of the sensational and investigations of the peripheral. The student of *David Copperfield* – or of any of the novels or stories for that matter – should first concentrate on the particular work in question; then he or she can turn to this study aid for critical explanations and commentaries.

Dickens was – and perhaps is, despite our turning away to media other than print – a national institution, the great fireside communicator of his own time and well into this century. But for many of us the fireside has gone, and the voices that speak to us are not rich in humanity or in social, moral or spiritual concern. Dickens is all these, and that is perhaps why we should read him so attentively today. For as we see Oliver ask for more; Dombey awaken to love for his daughter after the years of silent rejection; Pip's discovery of himself in his affection for Magwitch; or Lizzie Hexam's insistent sacrifice for her brother Charley's education, we touch the immutable fibres of human love beside which the computers and screens of our own time are ephemeral and irrelevant.

Plot and background

David is born after the death of his father and his early life is described. His mother re-marries (David having been sent to Yarmouth on holiday with his old nurse Peggotty) and David's home life is made miserable by his stepfather Mr Murdstone and the latter's sister Jane. Peggotty is always kind to him, and with his mother increasingly under the thumb of the Murdstones, David is sent away to school. There he is often unhappy, but he makes the acquaintance of and looks up to the most powerful boy in the school, James Steerforth.

On the death of his mother (she has a child which dies virtually at the same time), David is sent by Mr Murdstone to work in a warehouse in London. There he lodges with the financially impecunious Mr Micawber and his family. Eventually he can bear the work no longer, and runs away to Dover where he knows that his aunt Betsey Trotwood lives. She adopts him and sends him to a school run by Dr Strong in Canterbury. There he stays with Mr Wickfield and his daughter Agnes, and meets the ''umble' but cunning Uriah Heep. When he leaves school he goes up to London. By chance he meets Steerforth, and takes him on a holiday to the Peggottys at Yarmouth. Returned to London David is articled, through his aunt's money, to a firm of proctors working in Doctors' Commons. He falls in love with his employer's daughter, Dora Spenlow. Meanwhile Steerforth has carried off Mr Peggotty's niece Emily from Yarmouth, and Mr Peggotty determines to go in search of her. David's aunt Miss Trotwood has apparently lost her money, and David has to supplement his income. Meanwhile the cunning Uriah Heep has completely undermined Mr Wickfield, whose partner he becomes. He is also casting covetous eyes on Agnes.

David marries Dora some time after her father's death, and becomes a successful author; Dora proves to be spoilt and impratical, particularly when it comes to housekeeping. Some unjust suspicion of Dr Strong's wife having an affair with her cousin is cleared up. Emily has gone abroad with Steerforth, but she is eventually deserted by him; she comes to London and, through the agency of a girl she had befriended in the past, is found and taken care of by Mr Peggotty. Mr Micawber, who has been employed by Wickfield and Heep, exposes the villainy of the latter; through him the fortunes of Mr Wickfield and of Miss Trotwood are restored.

David's wife Dora dies, and Steerforth is drowned in a storm off Yarmouth. Mr Peggotty, Emily and the Micawbers emigrate to Australia. Some time after his wife's death David goes abroad for three years; when he returns he marries Agnes Wickfield, who has always loved him and for whom he has always had deep and loving feelings. Mr Peggotty returns home for a while and reports on the success of Micawber and the lives of the other emigrants, while David takes a final summarizing look at all the characters who have appeared in the history.

No summary can do justice to the texture of *David Copperfield* or to the richness of characterization and incident with which it is filled. A close study of the chapter commentaries as well as of the nature of Dickens's art will supply many of the omissions in the bald statements above. *David Copperfield* is a great novel primarily because of the sustained power of narrative emanating from the first-person teller, and his story is exciting, graphic, moving and compelling.

David Copperfield is a novel; it also contains many references which are identifiable in Dickens's own life. While these are interesting, and while sometimes we get the idea that these are imbued with a particularity of passion or sympathetic identification, we should *not* let them influence our evaluation of this novel as a work of art, because that is what a work of fiction, at least of a high order, is. D. H. Lawrence's *Sons and Lovers* (1913) and James Joyce's *A Portrait of the Artist as a Young Man* (1914–15) incorporate large but fictionalized slices of the authors' lives into their work. Dickens makes ready use of some of the most nostalgic or traumatic (or both) incidents of his own life, and these are given below for their own intrinsic interest. Do not confuse them with the printed text of *David Copperfield*, and if you make any reference to them do so in passing.

Dickens drew on his own experiences for the account of David's boyish church-going in Chapters 2 and 4, as well as the lessons he had from his mother (Chapter 4) and his clandestine reading of Smollett, Fielding etc. in the same chapter. There is little doubt that Mr Micawber is modelled *in part* on Dickens's father, a man of impecunious habits who was taken to the Marshalsea Prison in February 1824. The Dickens family was finally left to fend for itself in a bare house having pawned all their possessions. Micawber has Mr Dickens Snr's love of making punch and, like him, has a growing family. Mrs Dickens tried unsuccessfully, like Mrs Micawber, to set up a school. Perhaps the most important incident in Dickens's life, largely because of the psychological scar it left him with, came when he was sent to work in a blacking factory managed by his cousin James Lamert. It was his job to label blacking bottles with two other boys, Bob Fagin and Poll Green (note particularly the first name). He never forgot the experience and was tortured by the thought of his menial employment becoming known. When there was nothing left to pawn, the Dickens family went to live with their father in the Marshalsea, Charles lodging out and visiting the family in prison on Sundays. After three months John Dickens was released from prison; he had inherited a small legacy and made use of the Insolvent Debtors' Act. The parallels with the David/Micawber situation will have been noted. When his father was freed, Dickens was removed from the blacking factory and sent to school. The fictional differences and variants will also have been noted.

Dickens was twelve years old when he went to Wellington House Academy as a day-boy; the school was run by a Welshman who was much addicted to using the cane. Dickens was there for two years, then transferred to another school, leaving in 1827 to go into a lawyer's office as an office boy. Again, he did not find the work congenial, and he set to work to learn shorthand with the idea of becoming a parliamentary reporter. He had to make do with the position of shorthand writer at Doctors' Commons, but in 1832 he was employed as a parliamentary reporter in the gallery, working in that capacity first for the *Mirror of Parliament* and later for the *Morning Chronicle*. There are many adaptations in *David Copperfield*, with David (articled) being rather better placed than his creator in life.

In 1830, while Dickens was at Doctors' Commons, he fell in love with Maria Beadnell. This dominated his romantic life for the next three years, with Dickens often getting to Maria through her confidante, Mary Anne Leigh. In *David Copperfield* David marries his first love. Dickens did not, but his marriage was not a uniformly happy one, even early on. While he was working for the *Morning Chronicle* Dickens began to write stories under the pseudonym of 'Boz'. In Chapter 43 of the novel there is reference to David's early successes as a writer, and in Chapters 46 and 48 David refers to being engaged on a book which is such a success that he is able to give up reporting parliamentary debates. This parallels Dickens's own experience with the success of *Pickwick Papers*; by the end of 1836 he was able to devote himself to full-time writing, producing *Oliver Twist* concurrently with *Pickwick* and shortly afterwards starting on *Nicholas Nickleby*. In April

1836 Dickens married Catherine Hogarth; her sister Mary, whom Dickens greatly admired (and loved?) died in 1837. There is little doubt that the mental incompatibility of David and Dora derives in part from Dickens's own marital experience, while Agnes seems to have some connections – idealized of course – with Mary Hogarth. Finally, much of Dickens's work in the 1840s was done abroad, in 1844 in Italy, in 1846 in Switzerland, where he wrote *Dombey and Son*. The departure abroad after Dora's death finds David writing in Switzerland. As always, Dickens transforms life into the life of the imagination, and while we may delve the parallels, the differences are so marked as to make us wary of any positive identifications.

Chapter summaries, critical commentaries, textual notes and revision questions

Chapter 1

David gives some account of his birth (the reader has to suspend his disbelief about this, since David is only capable of recording what he has subsequently been told). His mother is sitting by the fire when her deceased husband's aunt, Miss Betsey Trotwood, appears. She announces that she will take care of the child when it is born, presuming throughout that it is going to be a girl. When she is proved wrong, she puts on her bonnet and walks out.

Commentary

Note the emphasis on the caul and the superstition attached to it, and David's self-humour about his own 'meandering'. He is already revealed as a very sensitive boy, pondering on the fact that his father never lived to see him. There is retrospect (a major technique in this novel, which is all retrospect in a sense) on Miss Trotwood, and a vivid presentation of her eccentricity. The essential weakness of Mrs Copperfield is seen and does not bode well for her future. The language is vivid with imaginative verve – 'like giants who were whispering secrets' – and resonant with subtle prophecy – 'like wrecks upon a stormy sea'. There are hints, despite her outwardly aggressive behaviour, of Miss Betsey's kindness. Notice how Mrs Copperfield's practice of keeping an account book is to be duplicated later in the David–Dora situation, another subtle psychological indication that David is later drawn to Dora because of her resemblance to his mother. There is some humour in the exchange between Betsey and Mr Chillip, and in the dramatic end to the chapter when Miss Betsey takes her abrupt leave.

a caul Part of the membrane enclosing the unborn child, sometimes found on the baby's head. It was considered to be a charm against death by drowning c.f. preferred 'cork jackets'.

Blunderstone Although Dickens saw the name or something close to it on a signpost, it has a strongly symbolic overtone of error and hardness, just as Murdstone has the same associations of hardness and the indelible mark of death.

two pair of stairs' i.e. up two flights of stairs.

Baboo ... Begum Hindu note of respect for (a) a clerk or the equivalent and (b) Indian woman of rank.

'a wax doll' Already the anticipation of Dora is evident in this phrase.

a Dutch clock A cheap clock of German make (Deutsch).

jeweller's cotton cotton wool.

the Ghost in *Hamlet* The dead King appears for the first time to his son in Act 1 Scene 4.

the national school Founded in 1811 by the National Society for Promoting the Education of the Poor in the Principles of the Established Church. Religion was the most important part of the curriculum.

the earthly bourne of all such travellers Another *Hamlet* association, this time from the famous soliloquy in which Hamlet ponders on the after life 'The undiscovered country, from whose bourne/No traveller returns ...'

Chapter 2

The recollections are of early childhood, with Peggotty and his mother very prominent. This is followed by Murdstone's courtship of Mrs Copperfield, David's relations with his mother and Peggotty (he asks the latter about marriage), and his suspicions of Murdstone, which he defines as 'uneasy jealousy'. Murdstone takes David on a day-trip to Lowestoft where he meets two of his friends; when he returns his mother is anxious to learn what has been said of her during the visit. Shortly afterwards it is arranged that David will go with Peggotty to Yarmouth for a fortnight, where they will stay with her brother.

Commentary

This chapter is full of the nostalgia and innocence of childhood, together with the affairs of the grown-ups which are to intimately affect David but of which he has no clear conception despite being christened 'Brooks of Sheffield' by the 'black' (and always black) Mr Murdstone. Notice the clarity of the prose which complements the clarity of the recollection of childhood. There is the sentimental attachment to the 'crocodiles', the fears of marriage which cause Davy to talk to Peggotty, and the latter's fears on Mrs Copperfield's account. Mrs Copperfield is vain and silly, easily flattered, and selfish (again think forward to Dora), while Peggotty is independent and has the nerve to confront her mistress with her dislike of Murdstone. The latter is an awesome man, apparently dead to all feelings (except for David's mother), and the innuendo with his friends is unpleasant.

Here Dickens works on two levels – the innocence of the boy and the clear indication to the reader what 'the projected business' is. The treat of the visit to Yarmouth is a transparent expedient, with the innocent boy now looking back and seeing his mother in her 'innocence' as she says goodbye to him. The child's love for his mother is not undermined by the omniscient irony.

how Lazarus was raised up from the dead See John 11, 43–4.
when affliction sore . . . Note the trite rhyming verse of the commemoration.
the little house . . . i.e. made in the shape of one.
Lawk An exclamation (Lord).
sensible Aware.
as stiff as a barrel Note the number of brief, effective metaphors and similes that Dickens employs.
shaver slang for 'young lad'.
'Brooks of Sheffield' i.e. very sharp, like a knife. Most cutlery was made in Sheffield.
broached the striking and adventurous proposition . . . i.e. the holiday in Yarmouth while 'the projected business' is undertaken.
a morsel of English Grammar pun on Ham's name = morsel of meat.
like the boy in the fairy-tale A reference to the tale of Hansel and Gretel in the *Fairy Tales* of the brothers Grimm.

Chapter 3

On arrival in Yarmouth Peggotty and David are met by Ham, who takes them to his home, the large boat-cum-barge left high and dry on the flat. The interior is described in detail, as well as the goodness of Mr Peggotty (a bachelor) to Mrs Gummidge, the widow of his former partner in the boat. He also adopted Ham and little Em'ly, his orphan nephew and niece in their childhood. David has a wonderful time and, childlike, falls in love with Em'ly, and suffers greatly when he has to go home. He suffers more on arrival, for he finds his mother married to Murdstone.

Commentary

The journey to Yarmouth is described with delightful humour and particularity, but the descriptions of individuals like Ham, Mr Peggotty and Mrs Gummidge take us into the genuine Dickensian mode of vivid pictorial and idiosyncratic detail. The description of the interior, with all its warmth and intimacy, reflects the warmth of the family connection and the goodness of Mr Peggotty. What is remarkable is the way Dickens captures the atmosphere and the susceptibility of childhood and its intense impressionability through the reactions of David. The smallness also reflects the smallness of the world which is to be largely crushed by the size of the outside world. David shows his inquisitiveness in his questioning of Mr Peggotty, but this underlines one of his characteristics, his interest in people which is later to turn him into a writer. There is more retrospect on Ham and Em'ly, pathetic in their case, but both humorous and poignant in the case of Mrs Gummidge. Already there is class awareness in Em'ly, and this in a way is an anticipation of her later downfall, since she wants to be a lady. That future fate is underlined in her near accident here and David's relief at her safety. Mrs Gummidge is superb, and Mr Peggotty's compassion is shown to be caring and practical. The ending of the chapter is moving as David is brought face to face with adult reality, and it is ominous too with the presence of Mr Murdstone.

a Yarmouth Bloater i.e. because Yarmouth is one of the chief ports in the herring fisheries.
'growed out of knowledge' i.e. beyond all belief.
caulkers' yards i.e. where the boats were repaired.
Aladdin's palace, roc's egg ... Indicative of David's (and Dickens's) familiarity with *The Arabian Nights*, where Aladdin has a large palace built through the magic of his lamp. The roc is the fabulous bird mentioned in the same tales, laying huge eggs.
smack Kiss.
she desired her compliments i.e. wished to be remembered to them.
fortnut Fortnight.
bacheldore Mr Peggotty's malapropism for 'bachelor'.
nankeen yellow cloth made of cotton (from Nanking in China).
That's why I should like so much to be a lady ... See the comments above, and study this passage carefully for anticipations of Em'ly's later fate.
Colosseum The famous amphitheatre in Rome built by the Emperor Vespasian in AD 72, and used for gladiatorial combats.
'The Willing Mind' Note the apt name of the pub, which is itself an ironic comment on the actions of some of the characters – like Mr Peggotty, Steerforth, Mrs Gummidge and, of course, David.
along of me Because of me.
a fit return i.e. repayment.
into the house The workhouse.
militia of words Note the image, evidence of Dickens's fertile imagination.
some shrubs that were dropping their heads ... Note this use of the

pathetic fallacy, where nature is in harmony – here miserable harmony – with the feelings of a character or characters.

Chapter 4

David is heartbroken. Mr Murdstone soon gives full indication of what their future relations are to be like, and with the arrival of Miss Murdstone things get worse. She takes over the running of the house, brushing aside the weak protestations of David's mother. His lessons are a torment, and his only solace is the secret reading of his father's books upstairs. One morning when he fails to learn what he is supposed to have learnt, Mr Murdstone takes the cane to him and David in spirited retaliation bites his hand. David is kept in his room for five days. Peggotty manages to communicate with him, and tells him that he is to be sent away to a school near London.

Commentary

This chapter is poignant with David's sufferings, with the weakness (and the spoiled nature) of his mother, with Peggotty's loyalty, and with the sadistic rule of the Murdstones. The jail imagery of Miss Murdstone's keys sufficiently indicates the prevailing atmosphere. David also has to watch his mother completely reduced and imprisoned by this hard, black, metallic pair. The description of the church-going is an underlining of the sombre and coercive atmosphere which prevails. There is little doubt that Dickens is attacking corporal punishment through the sufferings of David. Note also the movement from time to time into the present tense to make the torture more immediate. There is a brilliant focus on the child David's imaginative cravings as he becomes steeped in the books, but the atmosphere of tension is wrought to an intolerable pitch when David is about to be caned. The account and its aftermath are poignant in the extreme. David's confinement, with its terrible isolation, is also moving. The irony is that Clara finds herself blaming David for what has happened; in reality this is the measure of her own coercion.

Lord forgive you, Mrs Copperfield... The irony is that this parody of a prayer darkly anticipates the religiosity of the Murdstones.
very jail... heavy chain... like a bite Note the imagery, all redolent of prison and violence.
Wants manner i.e. lacks good manners.
base return Poor repayment.
tremendous visages i.e. severe expressions (on our faces).

the crocodile-book i.e. the symbol of happy times with Peggotty and his mother.
Mulatto Person of mixed race parentage, here tawny in colour.
a child once set in the midst of the Disciples Matthew 18,2 and Mark 9,36.
Roderick Random... The first three novels here are by Smollett (1721–71), who was a great influence on Dickens and one of the delights of his childhood reading – like David's.
Tom Jones The famous picaresque novel by Henry Fielding (1707–54). It was published in 1749, about 100 years before *David Copperfield*.
The Vicar of Wakefield (1766) by Oliver Goldsmith (1728–74).
Don Quixote (1605) The brilliantly satirical romance by the Spanish novelist and dramatist Cervantes (1547–1616).
Gil Blas Published 1715–35, by Le Sage, the French novelist and dramatist (1668–1747).
Robinson Crusoe (1719) by Daniel Defoe (1661–1731).
Arabian Nights The collection of Arabic Tales, first translated in the eighteenth century, and containing such stories as the adventures of Sinbad. A great favourite with Dickens.
Tales of the Genii An imitation of the *Arabian Nights* written by the Revd. James Ridley and published in 1765.
Tom Pipes The companion and servant of Peregrine Pickle in Smollett's novel of that name.
Strap Friend and servant to Roderick Random in Smollett's novel of that name.
Commodore Trunnion... Mr Pickle The latter is Peregrine's father, who spent his evenings at the pub with the eccentric naval officer Commodore Trunnion.
a good freshener... Irony. The sight of the cane puts David completely off.
a large linen wrapper i.e. a bandage.
It was a sort of comical affection... But note that it has an attendant pathos.

Chapter 5

David goes to Yarmouth with Mr Barkis, who asks him to send a message to Peggotty that 'Barkis is willin'. He does this at Yarmouth while waiting for the London coach, an obliging waiter helping him to eat his dinner. He arrives in London and is met by an assistant master at the school, Mr Mell. They visit the latter's mother (David suspects, and later finds out) in an almshouse, and from there they go to the school. This is deserted since the boys are on holiday. David works with Mr Mell. He is compelled to wear a placard on his back saying 'Take care of him, he bites'.

Commentary

The journey with Barkis is not only amusing, but contrasts with the imprisonment of the previous chapter. Ironically David's journey into life means that he is moving from domestic imprisonment to a wider one, though with the benefit of company and comradeship. The interaction with the opportunist waiter is also amusing. It is David's baptism into the larger world of swindling. Such is Dickens's emphasis that we are always made aware of David's size, and the waiter's morbid sense of humour has to be seen in moral relation to the small boy he is conning. The coach-journey to London gives adequate evidence of the insensitivity of adults to the child travelling with them. The atmosphere of isolation and loneliness predominates until the arrival of Mr Mell. The incident of the visit to the latter's mother again underlines the snobbery which is an important element in the plot not only in relation to Mr Mell, but through Steerforth and his affair with Little Em'ly. Loneliness gives way to the apprehensions roused by David's having to wear the badge of shame – Mr Murdstone's sadism follows David to Salem House.

come up i.e. get a move on.
parsties Pasties.
a set of casters A cruet.
six-foot i.e. a pun on David's diminutive size.
choker Scarf.
to come in and win i.e. beat him at showing how much he could eat.
cowpock i.e. suffering from small-pox.
pairint i.e. parent.
getting wind i.e. being spread about.
repelled the charge i.e. denied having been asleep.
They begin to close again . . . Note the use of the graphic present.
the groves of deserted bedsteads Note the mixed image – ironic in view of the fact that there is no evidence of nature here.
I picture . . . Note that the repetitions are a form of pathetic rhetoric.

Chapter 6

With the return of Mr Creakle, the headmaster, and his family, David is subjected to a harsh and terrifying interview. When the boys return from their holidays most are too dispirited to tease David. He learns much about the school and Mr Creakle's rule. An older boy, Steerforth, takes charge of David's seven shillings, and spends it on a moonlight supper for David and the other boys in his room. He assures David that he will take care of him.

Commentary

There is a neat contrast implied between the sadistic bully Creakle and his much softer wife and daughter, while the punch-voiced echo of the 'interpreter' provides a kind of sick commentary and comedy. Traddles immediately reveals his good nature, and Steerforth his authority, though at this stage his is a benevolent despotism. We note David's powers of observation and his dependence, and we recognize Steerforth's relation in terms of power to Mr Creakle. The poverty of the assistant teachers carries its own social (and moral) comment, but David shows his own brand of loyalty when he thinks of Mr Mell's secret.

Tartar i.e. a savage, from the brutality of the Tartar invaders of Eastern Europe.
Here's a game i.e. what about this!
prog Slang term for food.
a phosphorus-box An early development of the friction-match was the use of a sulphur-dipped splint with a box containing partially oxydized phosphorous.
the Borough i.e. the district in the city of London.
a set-off i.e. got his education for what his father charged for coal.
the table-beer was a robbery of parents i.e. it was watered down.
as poor as Job See *The Book of Job*, 1,14–22.
No veiled future . . . no shadowy picture Anticipatory hints that the future may yield something – as it does – which cannot at present be seen.

Chapter 7

The reign of terror in the schoolroom is described. Steerforth discovers that David knows many stories from the great novelists and gets him to tell these stories late each night and before they get up each morning. One day during a schoolroom mêlée Steerforth taunts Mr Mell with the fact that his mother lives in an almshouse. Creakle enters, takes Steerforth's part, and summarily dismisses Mr Mell. David receives a visit from Mr Peggotty and Ham at the school, and David introduces them to Steerforth. When the 'half' comes to an end, David goes home for the holiday.

Commentary

The atmosphere, with its emphasis on terror, fear and chaos, is described, all an abuse of what was done in the name of education. David the man is moved as he looks back at the physical and emotional sufferings he and the others endured, and the present tense is again used to convey the immediacy of the experiences. David himself shows his compassion, particularly towards the sufferings of Traddles, but his hero-worship of Steerforth is some compensation for David himself. Steerforth shows his romanticism and his indolence when he asks David to tell the stories, though these perhaps signal David's later capacity for story-telling when he himself becomes a writer. Steerforth's arrogance, insensitivity, snobbery and a streak of cruelty are evident in his treatment of Mr Mell. All our sympathies are with the downtrodden usher who is employed in a menial capacity and has no support from his master. Mell departs with dignity and shows a residuary kindness to David. Traddles shows his courage and his sense of fairness, while Steerforth displays that despicable characteristic which assumes that everything can be made right by money (he is to repeat this later with Little Em'ly). The visit of Ham and Mr Peggotty has a certain naiveté and goodness about it. It is important to the plot, since it points Steerforth in their direction.

mouths Grimaces.
like the Sultana Scheherazade The fictitious narrator of the stories of the *Arabian Nights*. The Sultan decided to marry a new wife each evening, and to strangle each one in the morning to prevent her unfaithfulness. Scheherazade married him but saved her own life by telling him tales each night which kept his interest in suspense until their continuation on the following night.
roopy Hoarse.
stomachic i.e. medicine to help the digestion.
Alguazil An inferior magistrate or police sergeant in Spain.
bruited Noised abroad, advertised.
kept the house from indisposition Stayed indoors ill.
Polly i.e. you are as foolish as a parrot, which can only repeat.
bor' Boy.
merry-go-rounder i.e. a celebration.
you might see it anywheres i.e. however bad the light.
my endeavours i.e. my very best.
pound i.e. be bound.
six chapters of Greek Testament i.e. translation of the New Testament Greek.
giving it Beating.

Chapter 8

David is brought home to Blunderstone by Barkis, who asks him to tell Peggotty that he is waiting for an answer. When he arrives he finds that the Murdstones have gone out for the day. He discovers that he now has a baby brother, and spends a delightful afternoon and evening with his mother and Peggotty. But in the evening the Murdstones return bringing their own constraint with them. David spends a miserable month at home and is almost glad when the holidays are over and he can go back to school.

Commentary

The early amusement of this chapter lies in the fact that Barkis is as ever willing and David becomes the innocent go-between. Note the ironic title of the chapter, since 'holidays' are the last things one would associate with the Murdstones. There is a sense of change to follow the transitory happiness, already a pathos about the baby, though the shyness, delight and loyalty of Peggotty are uplifting. There is an atmosphere of impending doom, with time snatched in a vacuum before the return of the Murdstones. Peggotty initiates talk of Miss Trotwood, almost as if she knows intuitively what is to happen in the future. The recurrence to the Crocodile Book is an attempt to recapture the happiness of earlier childhood. The loneliness and the coercion (and the injustice) are terrible to contemplate, while David's picture of the farewell to his mother has all the factual and symbolic effects of a last goodbye, which indeed it is.

The bare old elm trees wrung their many hands . . . The personification effectively contributes to the desponding atmosphere.
for all the world and his wife i.e. anybody.
some Cats i.e. Miss Murdstone.
the last of its race i.e. of happiness.
interdicted Forbidden.
daymare An imaginative equivalent to 'nightmare'.
Rule Britannia,* or *Away with Melancholy The first is the celebrated popular song, music by Dr Arne (1710–78) and words by James Thomson (1700–48), the second is a song adapted from the music of Mozart.
threading my grandmother's needle A term from a contemporary party game.

Chapter 9

After he has been back at school for a couple of months, David receives the news from Mrs Creakle that his mother has died. He goes home for the funeral, and is met at Yarmouth by Mr Omer the undertaker and his family. The funeral is described, David's mother being buried with her baby, which only survived her by one day, and afterwards Peggotty tells David how his mother came to die.

Commentary

It is typical of Dickens, or rather the Dickensian irony, that David's birthday should coincide with the death of his mother. David's reactions are movingly those of a deprived child, but there is a wonderful insight into the importance such grief confers upon the griever. The interlude at Mr Omer's has all the practicality of preparation. The mechanical carrying through of the funeral again finds David lonely and cut off, but before that we are made aware that Mr Murdstone *is* moved by his wife's death so that he becomes, in our eyes, something of a more rounded character. But Peggotty's narrative of his mother's words to her at least bring David back into the orbit of warmth, love, and concern.

gay i.e. happy, light-hearted, with none of the modern associations of the word.
chaise Light open horse-drawn carriage.
half pianoforte van i.e. for transporting pianos.
bait Feed.
a byegone i.e. all over.

Chapter 10

Peggotty is given a month's notice by Miss Murdstone. She tries to get a local position, fails, but is permitted to take David for a holiday to Yarmouth. There he renews his friendship with Little Em'ly and the others, and towards the end of his stay Peggotty and Barkis are married. He tells his friends all about Steerforth. When he returns home he finds that the Murdstones don't want his company – perhaps it is that Mr Murdstone now has less money. However Mr Quinion, a partner of Murdstone's, reappears, and David learns that he is to start work at Murdstone and Grinby's, the wine business with which Mr Murdstone is connected.

Commentary

The closeness of David and Peggotty is stressed, and Peggotty is now cut off from all the associations which have made the best part of her life. The atmosphere is lightened by the advances of Barkis both on the journey and afterwards. The marriage keeps Peggotty near her roots in Blunderstone. David's first view of Em'ly is sensitively described ('a curious feeling came over me that made me pretend not to know her', p.140), and there is a delightful interchange of teasing between them. There is some emphasis on the fact that Em'ly is spoiled by them all, and a terrible irony in David's praise of Steerforth in view of the fact that he is going to cause them all such misery. Note also the delighful innocence and humour about the wedding-day. David indulges his capacity for dreaming by thinking of himself and Little Em'ly, again ironic, since fate is writing a different story. The return home provides the terrible contrast of reality after the holiday idyll.

a suitable service i.e. a job.
wearing out the ring in my pocket i.e. because it has been there so long.
Rudderford A typical Mr Peggotty association, redolent of the sea.
in the way of book-larning ... This assumption about Steerforth helps to establish an image which belies his character.
he's such a generous, fine, noble fellow ... David's blindness is here evident, but every adjective is a stroke of irony.
betimes Early.
chaise-cart See note p.23.
Rhoeshus Barkis's pronunciation of Roscius, the famous Roman comic actor (died 62 BC). He is paying David a compliment.
Foxe's Book of Martyrs By John Foxe (1516–87), published in Latin in 1559, printed in English 1563. It is a history of the church with special reference to the sufferings of the martyrs, largely Protestant ones, and is an indictment of Papism.

Chapter 11

David begins work at Murdstone and Grinby's in London. He washes and labels bottles, describes his way of life and remuneration, and is introduced to Mr Micawber, with whom he is to lodge. Mr Micawber, whose lifestyle is characterized by perpetual insolvency, has to go into the King's Bench Prison for debt. When all the remaining household effects have been pawned, the rest of the family join him there. In the prison Mr Micawber draws up a petition to the House of Commons praying for an alteration in the law of imprisonment for debt.

Commentary

The early account here is tinged with autobiographical bitterness. But note the explicitness of the account and the narrative interest aroused with the descriptions of the other boys and of the working conditions. The atmosphere lifts with the arrival of Mr Micawber, one of the most brilliant characters in the Dickensian galaxy. He is initially bent on making an impression, and consequently uses high-sounding phrases. These become something of an index to his insecurity. The family are a delight, with Mrs Micawber having come down in the world but determined never to desert Mr Micawber. Again there is the autobiographical element, with Mrs Micawber trying to found a school, just as Dickens's mother had done in fact. There is some wonderful graphic humour as Mr Micawber's creditors try to close with him, but best of all are the sudden transitions from despair to euphoria which characterize husband and wife. David's own recollections of his smallness in the adult world are poignant; his concern for the Micawbers shows his need of family warmth. The poverty and pawning sequence is a comment on social conditions, the interior of the debtors' prison a documentation of them. Always we are aware of David's sense of degradation in his job and, insistently, of the London which surrounds him. The petition and the organization of it is fine mock ceremony.

did Imps in the Pantomimes An indication, and there are many, of Dickens's love of the theatrical.

a brown surtout and black tights A frock-coat and tight-fitting trousers of the period.

your peregrinations in this metropolis... Typical high-flown language of Micawber when he wants to make an impression.

the arcana of the Modern Babylon i.e. the mysteries and secrets of London.

a turn at a neighbouring pump i.e. washed myself at a communal tap.

'a Orfling' An orphan.

experientia does it The Latin is *experientia docet* – experience teaches.

execution i.e. a seizure of goods.

Jack's delight being his lovely Nan The song *Lovely Nan* by Charles Dibdin (1745–1814).

in case anything turned up The phrase associated with the incurable Micawber optimism.

a pair of sugars i.e. sugar-tongs.

the King's Bench Prison The old established debtors' prison in Borough High Street which allowed prisoners to live within three miles of it and to buy periods of liberty. What is recounted here is based on Dickens's

26 David Copperfield

father's experiences; there is a comparable treatment of the Dorrit family's life in the Marshalsea in *Little Dorrit* (1855–7).

a written order i.e. a promise to pay.

a little jug of egg-hot Hot beer or cider with eggs beaten up in it.

casino A popular card game in the early 19th century.

demoniacal parchments ... Germany A reference to Faust's compact with the Devil to sell him his soul. See Marlowe's *Dr Faustus* and Goethe's *Faust*.

the Insolvent Debtors' Act Whereby the private (not the trading) debtor could get himself released from prison providing that he promised to pay. Mr Dickens got his release by this means from the Marshalsea in 1824.

Chapter 12

Mr Micawber is discharged from the Debtors' Prison, and leaves London for Plymouth, where he has hopes that something may 'turn up'. David sees the family off. His adopted family gone, he decides to run away from Murdstone and Grinby's to seek out his only relative, Miss Betsey Trotwood. Without disclosing his intention, he learns from Peggotty that his aunt lives at Dover. He has a brush with a young man who steals his box and the half-guinea given to him by Peggotty. He thus has nothing to pay for his fare, and sets out on the Dover Road to walk the distance.

Commentary

There is the now familiar comedy of the Micawbers with Mrs Micawber going into a dramatic faint, and David notes that they are only happy when they have their troubles with them. They show their great affection for David though. Mr Micawber gives him the classic advice which is so often quoted (see p. 175 of the Pan edition) in which the overspending of a fraction is the difference between misery and happiness. There is a wonderful moment at the parting when Mrs Micawber appears motherly to the small waif who is David Copperfield. The incident with the young man indeed emphasizes David's lack of stature. It is grotesque, a sick joke, like so many aspects of life.

harmonic meeting i.e. a sing song.

flip See note on 'egg-hot'.

taking a chair on the staircase i.e. sitting outside.

the strangers' bell i.e. indicating that visitors should leave.

some new shift i.e. having to move (into another lodging).

without warrant i.e. lightly.

disbanded Sacked.
Collar him i.e. time – act quickly.
'Take him for all in all, we ne'er shall . . .' Mr Micawber is quoting Hamlet's description of his father (*Hamlet*, Act 1, Scene 2, lines 186–7).
Annual income . . . The blossom is blighted . . . Note that the practical advice is followed by the poetic embellishment, typical of Mr Micawber's mode of speaking.
the Obelisk A memorial to a Lord Mayor. It was built in 1771.
warmin Vermin, scoundrel.

Revision questions on Chapters 1–12

1 Write an account of the most moving incident in David's childhood.

2 Write character sketches of any two of the following: (a) Mr Peggotty; (b) Ham; (c) Mrs Gummidge; (d) Mrs Micawber; (e) Miss Murdstone.

3 Indicate the role played by Peggotty in David's life so far, bringing out clearly her main characteristics.

4 Compare and contrast the two holidays which David spends at Yarmouth.

5 Compare David's life at home after his mother's marriage to his 'first half' at Salem House.

6 What do you consider to be the nature of Dickens's humour in the novel so far? Write an essay on it, bringing out the main elements as clearly as you can.

7 'A breath of light.' How far does this brief description of Mr Micawber indicate his influence on David.

8 'He is too sorry for himself.' Is this a fair description of David?

Chapter 13

The account of David's six-day journey along the Dover Road. It is an endurance test, for he passes by Salem House in Blackheath and goes on through Rochester, Chatham and Canterbury, selling his jacket and waistcoat in order to provide himself with the necessities of life. In Dover he finds Miss Trotwood's house, and presents himself to her in his deplorable condition. He tells her his story to Miss Trotwood and she sees to it that David has a bath and is fed. Whenever she wants advice about what to do, she consults Mr Dick, and always uses him as the measure of common-sense.

Commentary

David learns about commercial life the hard way, and once more we feel the pathos of his situation. Again we note the isolation of David, and the irony of his being outside Salem House, almost a landmark here of his past security and snatched happiness. The meeting with the madman is frightening, that with the tinker imbued with fear and violence. Miss Betsey, as we might expect, is a real eccentric, and her consultation with Mr Dick belies her uncertainty. Nevertheless, like Mr Micawber, her very nature brings a considerable lifting of the heavy atmosphere. Note the imposing character of Miss Betsey but the stress on the neatness of her home which is complimentary to herself and to Janet. The donkey-phobia is of course natural comedy – Miss Betsey is a rare one for obsessions – and the gentle Mr Dick is a natural foil to her. With her strong views she is still touched by David's defence of Peggotty. The chapter ends on a note of poignancy as David finds himself in the comfort of the bedroom and feels the sense of family which he has craved for for so long.

a scrap of newspaper intelligence i.e. an item of news.
slop-shops i.e. selling ready-made and second-hand clothes.
The Death of Nelson A popular song by S. J. Arnold (1774–1852) with words by John Braham.
What lay . . .? i.e. what's your game/job? What's your line of business?
prig slang for 'thief'.
fly-drivers i.e. those driving carriages with four wheels pulled by a single horse.
like a tollman's apron The toll-gate keeper who wore an apron with a pocket in which he kept his change.
expressly to educate in a renouncement of mankind i.e. she had trained them up to hate men.
marries a Murderer . . . Deliberate distortion by Betsey, but not without ironic application to Murdstone, who murdered the spirit and may well have hastened his wife's death by his insensitivity.
He's as like Cain . . . i.e. the kind of person who looks as if he might become a murderer (see Genesis, 4,5).

Chapter 14

Betsey determines to write a letter to Mr Murdstone about what has happened. Betsey gives an account of Mr Dick's career and how his family have treated him. When the Murdstones arrive it becomes clear that they are intent upon blackening David and disclaiming responsibility for him if he stays with his aunt. Betsey tells them her opinion of their behaviour in relation to David (and indeed his mother) in no uncertain terms, and they leave having been verbally trounced by that lady. She keeps David, deciding to give him her name of Trotwood.

Commentary

The reader's suspicions that Betsey has a heart of gold under her stern exterior are confirmed in this chapter. Firstly we have her obvious concern, compassion and genuine feeling (and activity on his behalf) for Mr Dick. Secondly, there is her rigorous and unflinching putting down of the Murdstones. Before that we are made aware of the idiosyncratic simplicity of Mr Dick. The latter is a kind man who soon becomes very attached to David. There is a fine irony in his presentation, since he who considers the world mad is in fact thought to be so by the world. He is seen by his narrator (and of course by Betsey) with a loving compassion. We are moved by David's anguish at the thought of being returned to the Murdstones. However, Betsey humiliates Mr Murdstone verbally and achieves a like effect with Miss Murdstone by skillfully ignoring her. Mr Dick's idea of having David measured for a suit provides a fitting anti-climax to the acrid exchange with the Murdstones.

Phoebus The sun or sun-god in Greek mythology – here used without apparent innuendo by Mr Dick.
it's a mad world . . . Bedlam The phrase was first popularized by Nicholas Breton in the Elizabethan era. Bedlam is the shortened name for the Bethlehem Hospital, a lunatic asylum in London which had formerly been a religious house.
a natural i.e. an idiot.
his allegorical way i.e. this is the way in which he thinks of it.
King Charles the First Ruled from 1625 until his execution in 1649.
Franklin Benjamin Franklin (1706–90), the American diplomatist and scientist. He experimented with kites and through them demonstrated that lightning was an electrical phenomenon. He was not a Quaker but a freethinker.
habiliments Clothes.
battle-piece i.e. a picture of strife.
bespoke Ordered.

Chapter 15

David flies the kite with Mr Dick, who is obviously glad of his companionship. Betsey suggests that 'Trot', as he is now called, shall go to school, and she takes him to Canterbury. They enquire at the house of Mr Wickfield, his aunt's lawyer, for the best school; and it is arranged that, as she did not approve of any of the boarding houses proposed for him, David should live with Mr Wickfield and his daughter Agnes. David catches a glimpse of Uriah Heep.

Commentary

David is embraced by the feeling of compassion and enjoyment as he becomes friendly with Mr Dick. He begins to feel more self-important and self-confident at the prospect of school. His dignity as an individual is beginning to be restored. Throughout the kindness, support and love of Betsey Trotwood are evident; she is in effect a surrogate mother to 'Trotwood', as her bestowing this name upon him indicates. Important plot indications are evident in the introduction of Uriah Heep, with the unsavoury atmosphere which he generates; the port-wine associations with Mr Wickfield, a hint at the habit which is to bring him down and put him in Heep's power; and, of course, the ministering angel Agnes, who is seen without irony. There is considerable expectation aroused at the close of this instalment (number 5), with David's going to school again the start of a new life but with the shadow of Uriah Heep beginning to impress itself on his (and our) consciousness.

evolutions i.e. speed of thought and decision.
plain dealer Honest man.

Chapter 16

David goes with Mr Wickfield to the school where he meets Dr Strong. Soon he notices his young wife Annie, and hears Dr Strong and Wickfield talk about his wife's cousin, Jack Maldon. Dr Strong wishes to make provision for him. David reveals his reactions to being in school again, and also talks to Agnes, who is effectively her father's housekeeper. Maldon is introduced by Heep and seems resigned to going abroad. Later Wickfield, who has drunk much wine, asks David if he wishes to stay with them. It is decided that he will. He has some conversation with Uriah Heep, who hopes eventually to receive his articles as a lawyer, but who constantly reiterates his 'umbleness'. His 'writhing' disconcerts David. There follows a description of the school and the fact that Dr Strong is much liked. David delights in Strong's mother-in-law Mrs Markleham, who persists in going back over the doctor's marriage proposal to Annie. Jack Maldon leaves to go abroad, and Annie is found afterwards in a fainting fit on the floor.

Commentary

The initial emphasis is on the Maldon part of the plot and on Wickfield's suspicions of an affair between Maldon and Annie. David is intent on concealing his past in the wine warehouse, but he soon comes to know Agnes, who even at this stage appears to be idealized through her devotion to her father. Maldon gives the impression of being rather a stagey villain. Wickfield obviously wants David to stay, but takes it to heart when he feels that his daughter may find his constant companionship dull. Wickfield is a disturbed man. The transition to Heep is ominous, and we feel at once that he is plotting on his own account despite his 'umbleness', and that he may well have his eyes on Agnes. David shows his resilience by adapting well to school, which he had feared because of his background, and the goodness of the doctor is given a considered stress. A mystery is set up over the constraint between Wickfield and Annie, while Mrs Markleham – the Old Soldier – is a Dickensian humorous grotesque in the best manner, garrulous and dominating. Her statements almost invite us to think, though not directly, that there is an affair between Annie and Jack Maldon. The cherry-coloured bow symbolizes the idea that Annie and Jack are lovers, and the fainting-fit is the apparent confirmation.

like sublimated skittles Note the small vividness of the image.
Doctor Watts ... Satan finds some mischief ... The quotation is from *Against Evil Company* in the *Divine Songs for Children* by Isaac Watts (1674–1748), the Non-conformist preacher who wrote, among others, *O God our Help in Ages Past*.
Tidd's Practice William Tidd (1760–1847, a famous legal writer, chiefly known for his *Practice of the Court of King's Bench* (1790–94). He was for some years the sole authority for common law practice.
a pale, inexpressive-faced watch Note how the personification of the watch complements the nature of Heep.
botanical furor David's joke on himself and at the Doctor's obsession with grammar.

Old Soldier . . . her generalship . . . marshalled great forces Notice
how Dickens uses a consistent image to define her conversational flow.
Hindoo i.e. anything Indian.
Sindbad i.e. Sindbad the Sailor, hero of the story of the same name in the
Arabian Nights, who enjoyed some wonderful adventures on his sea voyages.

Chapter 17

David keeps up a correspondence with Peggotty. Mr Dick pays him fortnightly visits to Canterbury and on one such occasion has a strange story to tell – that of a mysterious man who hides near Miss Betsey's house at Dover and frightens her. Mr Dick becomes very popular at the school. Meanwhile David goes to tea with Uriah Heep, where he is systematically questioned about Mr Wickfield's affairs and his own. While he is there Mr Micawber appears unexpectedly and David introduces him to the Heeps. Mrs Micawber explains how the family come to be in Canterbury. Later David notices that Uriah Heep has attached himself to Mr Micawber. The Micawbers invite David to dinner; next morning he receives a most desperate letter from Mr Micawber. The Micawbers depart for London.

Commentary

For David there is the delight of news from Peggotty (though he is saddened that his old home is shut up following the departure of the Murdstones). Mr Dick brings the serious news of the mysterious stranger (Dickens loves a mystery, and well knows that it sells numbers). There is something both sad and happy about the boy that Mr Dick becomes when he visits David, and that poignancy is extended to his adulation of the doctor, 'enchained by interest, with his poor wits calmly wandering God knows where, upon the wings of hard words'. The interview with the Heeps is grotesque, particularly as David finds Mrs Heep still in mourning, but it is also ominous with the overtones of potential blackmail. Another dramatic note is struck with the arrival of Mr Micawber, and not the least of David's worries is that he will reveal the past, which he almost does by his reference to the wine trade. Nevertheless the re-introduction of the Micawbers provides the reader with the opportunity to contemplate the problems of their 'pecuniary obligations' anew. Their real appeal is that they have not changed. There is unease for David as he sees Micawber with Heep – a very important plot move this – but the little dinner is followed by the contrast of the now expected suicidal letter, followed in turn by David seeing the family, in very good heart, off to London.

crampbones Sheep's kneebones, thought to be a preventive of cramp.
escritoire Writing desk.
vomiting papers Notice the expressiveness of the image, part of Dickens's vivid style.
weeds i.e. widow's mourning.
A tender young cork ... a pair of corkscrews Note again the vividness and imagination of the imagery.
a touch of nature i.e. made them almost normal.
touch of art i.e. they contrived everything they did.
a succession of facers i.e. a number of effective blows.
in the words of Cato ... The quotation is 'It must be so – Cato, thou reasonest well' from *Cato* (Act 5, Scene 1), a tragedy by Joseph Addison (1672–1719) which was published in 1713. This is an apt reference, since the play tells the story of Cato's last days; he commits suicide rather than surrender to Caesar.
Medway Coal Trade Coal for the Medway towns was brought by sea and sold in Kent.
'Auld Lang Syne' The famous song by the great Scottish poet Robert Burns (1759–96). The two quotations, the first one slightly altered, come from the last stanza: 'a right gude Willie Waught' means a good draught or drink.
The bolt is impending ... i.e. the thunderbolt, fate. Typical of the extreme of Mr Micawber's mood.

Chapter 18

This narrative is really an account of David's life at Canterbury, and consists of a series of incidents – his young love for Miss Shepherd, his fight, in which he comes off worst, with a young butcher, and his becoming head boy of the school. By now Agnes is grown up. David describes his boyish infatuation for the eldest Miss Larkins.

Commentary

The dancing school interlude is delightfully expressed, in fact one feels that this chapter is in some ways a hint of David's future profession of author, so graphically are the various incidents described. There is, perhaps unconsciously, in David's epic battle with the butcher's boy an echo of the Cuff v Dobbin fight in *Vanity Fair*, which was issued a year or so before the publication of *David Copperfield*. David is essentially romantic (his feelings for Miss Larkins anticipate the complete obsession later with Dora), while the end of the chapter is masterly – Miss Larkins being engaged to the older man rather than the dashing captain. David has the capacity to laugh at himself.

spencer A short overcoat (so named from the Earl Spencer (1758–1834) who made this kind of coat popular.)
in the stocks This was a device used in girls' boarding schools for straightening the feet.
like the apparition of an armed head in Macbeth See *Macbeth* 4, 1, 68 where his own fate, to be killed by Macduff, is forecast.
spoony Romantic.
expire Die (David is being romantically melodramatic).
bears grease Fat from the bear used to grease the hair.

Chapter 19

David leaves the school at Christmas, and Betsey suggests that he has a holiday with Peggotty at Yarmouth before he decides what career he will pursue. He has a worrying conversation with Agnes about the deterioration of her father and of the part that Heep appears to be playing in this. David is now very observant, and at Dr Strong's he learns of Jack Maldon's wish to return from India. He further notices that Mr Wickfield appears to be suspicious of Mrs Strong. He sets out for Yarmouth, going to London by coach and, on returning to an inn after visiting the Covent Garden theatre, he unexpectedly meets Steerforth in the coffee room. He learns that Steerforth is now a student at Oxford.

Commentary

David shows a seriousness of intention as he determines to make his way in the world, and a fitting recognition of what Betsey has done for him. We note her insistent sense of morality. David's first visit deepens his intimacy with Agnes and their joint concern for her father. The sub-plot involving Annie and Jack Maldon deepens, and the comments of the Old Soldier are calculated to create trouble. David's own thoughts are restless in this direction. This in part accounts for his blindness in relation to Agnes. He suffers some humiliation at relinquishing his advantageous position on the coach, and is now once more made aware of his youth. David is always self-conscious about this. Note how impressionable he is about the visit to the theatre, and how his need is met, to be recognized and accepted, when he sees a somewhat condescending Steerforth.

like a couple of knaves Probably a pair of these in a game of cards.
contract-bargain It is phrases like this that make David suspicious – and Wickfield – that the Doctor has in his goodness resigned himself to the fact that his wife prefers her cousin Jack Maldon to an old man like himself.
remarked Noticed.
Suffolk Punch A breed of heavy draught horses with short legs and thick-set body and neck.
pound it i.e. swear to it.
I felt as if the tinker's hand... David is extremely sensitive, and this humiliation reminds him of an earlier one on the road to Dover.
taters Potatoes.
link-lighted... patten-clinking Note how Dickens immediately creates the atmosphere of the busy London street with the link-boys lighting the way for passengers and the noise of the shoes on the pavements.
Daisy The nickname points to David's innocence, which is to be fully exploited.

Chapter 20

After breakfasting with Steerforth, David is invited to spend a day or two with him at his home in Highgate. Steerforth tells him that he has no intention of taking a degree at Oxford. David now meets Mrs Steerforth and her companion Rosa Dartle, and is thrilled when Steerforth intimates that he may go with him on his visit to the Peggottys. Although he learns how Rosa Dartle has come by her scar, his devotion to Steerforth, his almost unqualified admiration for him, is undiminished. This love and admiration is of course shared by Mrs Steerforth.

Commentary

Steerforth has a private apartment at the inn, a measure of his power, position and money which we later see have done so much to corrupt him. His natural indolence is shown in his admitted incapacity to work for a degree. The immediate impact made by Rosa Dartle is disconcerting and makes for unease. She is depicted through vivid imagery ('She was a little dilapidated – like a house – with having been so long to let') while Mrs Steerforth is in the ironic position of being a doting mother who misguidedly thinks that her son will apply himself to work while at college. Rosa Dartle's innuendoes are viperish, calculated to undermine. Notice Steerforth's condescension ('to see that sort of people together') and his complete ignorance of human nature ('they have not very fine natures . . . they are not easily wounded'). Compare the adoption of Rosa by Mrs Steerforth with that of Ham and Em'ly by Peggotty. We note that Steerforth has been overindulged, and that David is a dupe in his company. The chapter ends on a markedly symbolic note with David seeing the scarless portrait of Rosa Dartle. He himself provides the scar, and that scar symbolizes the capacity to wound indelibly which Steerforth possesses.

King Charles on horseback i.e. the statue.
the lions i.e. the sights of the town.
a Panorama a mechanically produced show, a picture of a landscape or other view unrolled before or revolving round the spectator so that he appears to be passing the various scenes depicted.
the Museum i.e. the British Museum in Great Russell Street.
on all hands Everywhere.
the lilies of the valley A quotation which has been adapted from Matthew, 6,28.

Chapter 21

There is a description of Littimer, Steerforth's servant, and the monotony of his conversation and practices. David has riding lessons during his stay. Then they go down to Yarmouth, where David renews his acquaintance with Mr Omer, who gives him the news that Em'ly is apprenticed as a dressmaker in his establishment. Peggotty is of course overjoyed to see David, as is Barkis. David and Steerforth have dinner at Peggotty's and later go on to see Peggotty's house. There they find a celebration going on to mark the engagement of Little Em'ly and Ham. Steerforth charms everybody with his friendly and open behaviour.

Commentary

We note the effect on David of Littimer, a hint about his later importance in the plot. David is so susceptible to Steerforth's good opinion that he is pleased when he praises Yarmouth. The superb brief description of the day and the sea reflects the optimism and happiness of David's mood. We learn that Em'ly's attractions excite jealousy in other women and ironically (in view of the plot) 'that

Em'ly wanted to be a lady'. There is some wonderful humour in Peggotty's gradually recognizing David, and pathos attends Barkis and his crippling rheumatism. David the man has one terrible moment of looking back with the hindsight – which the reader does not possess – of knowing what has happened, aware that at the time Steerforth was passing an idle hour – 'this was a brilliant game, played for the excitement of the moment'. His indolent sophistication contrasts with the warmth of Mr Peggotty and the scene which they interrupt. Again we are aware of structure – of the Ham/Em'ly engagement in some ways approximating in its unevenness to that of Dr Strong and Annie, not in years here but in capacity. Mr Peggotty's story of the engagement, particularly as narrated to the opportunist Steerforth, shows his trustingly simple nature. It contrasts tellingly with Steerforth, who refers to Ham as 'rather a chuckle-headed fellow for the girl' (p. 316). It is followed by a rare display of conscience from Steerforth when he notes that David is shocked in earnest; he adds in a moment of dramatic character-revelation 'I wish we all were' (p. 316).

tarpaulin Sailor.
rollers Waves.
the murder's out i.e. the secret is revealed.
When the stormy winds do blow ... The refrain occurs at the end of each stanza of *Ye Mariners of England*, by Thomas Campbell (1777–1844).
Hollands A spirit manufactured from grain in Holland – gin.
chuckle-headed Stupid.

Chapter 22

David goes over to Blunderstone several times, and on returning from his last visit comes across Steerforth sitting alone at Mr Peggotty's in a very dejected state. As they walk to the inn Steerforth confides in David that he has bought a boat which he intends to call 'The Little Em'ly'. They meet Ham and Em'ly, who are being followed by a girl. David meets the extraordinary Miss Mowcher, who calls at the inn to see Steerforth. When he returns to Mr Barkis's house, David hears about Martha from Ham. He sees Em'ly tending her. Em'ly is overcome by tears, and tells Ham that she is unworthy of him.

Commentary

We note David's capacity for a nostalgic indulgence of the past and his balancing dreams about making a name for himself in the future.

There is a kind of irony in the fact that David's old home is now occupied by a lunatic. David's finding Steerforth depressed is a hint of what is to come, for Steerforth is momentarily overcome by his conscience. At the same time he admits that he has taken a liking to the place. The naming of the boat causes Steerforth some embarrassment, almost as if he feels that David may suspect his motives. The plot is given something of a melodramatic flavour with the introduction of the mystery woman following Ham and Em'ly. This is redeemed by the introduction of the grotesque Miss Mowcher, who has a wonderful colloquial grasp and is intent on gossip as well as her art. She also has a kind of running flirtatiousness which is endearing. She is sharp, particularly when she scents romance. Steerforth reveals, perhaps unconsciously, the way his thoughts are working when he observes of Em'ly 'I swear she was born to be a lady' (p. 331). That he is intent on seduction is obviously understood by Miss Mowcher. The presence of Martha as a fallen woman leads to a somewhat stagey scene, but Em'ly shows that she has a conscience about what she is doing unbeknown to anyone when she bursts out 'I am not as good a girl as I ought to be.'

weazen Wizened, very small.
mongrel time i.e. that is neither one thing nor the other.
'Why being gone ... with most admired disorder Both the quotations are from *Macbeth* Act 3, Scene 4.
binding ... the Ixions of these days Ixion in Greek mythology was punished by Zeus for his treachery by being banished to Hades and there 'bound' to a revolving wheel. Steerforth is saying that he avoids any permanent work.
downy wide-awake (Slang).
Hookey estates 'Hookey Walker' was a slang term for disbelief and mistrust.
gammon and spinnage Humbug and deception.
a broth of a boy i.e. quite a lad, you think well of yourself.
Madagascar Liquid Her way of referring to Macassar oil, a popular hair-dressing.
Griffin A fabulous monster with a lion's body and eagle's head and wings.
Did he sip ... requited? A quotation from Macheath's song in John Gay's *The Beggar's Opera* (1728).
a rattle An incessant talker.
Fatima From the story of Bluebeard, by Charles Perrault (1628–1703). Bluebeard has married a number of wives, each of whom has disappeared. He eventually marries Fatima. She unlocks a forbidden room while he is away and finds the bodies of the previous wives. Bluebeard is killed before he can kill her.

noddle i.e. head.
mizzle Clear off.
Let's get the scaffolding up i.e. let's make the preparations.
like a goblin pie-man Note the grotesque, almost fairy-tale suggestions here.
Ned Beadwood a character in an old song.
Jocky of Norfolk From Shakespeare's *Richard III*, Act 5 Scene 3, line 305.
"Bob swore" Miss Mowcher's pronunciation of 'Bon soir', French for 'Good evening'.
long-headed i.e. sharp, not missing a point.
a scientific cupper i.e. able to draw blood from a patient by means of a cupping glass. Bleeding was often used in cases of illness, and often undertaken by barbers, hence the red stripe in the barber's pole.
wurem Worm.

Chapter 23

On the way back to London David consults Steerforth on his aunt's suggestion that he should become a proctor. Steerforth defines this profession for him. David meets his aunt in London. On their way to Doctors' Commons she recognizes a rough-looking man with whom she disappears, only to return without the guineas she had in her purse. She offers no explanation, but David remembers the account given by Mr Dick of the rough-looking man who hung about the house (Chapter 17). They meet Mr Spenlow in his office and it is arranged that David shall be articled to Spenlow and Jorkins. Later Betsey arranges rooms for David at Mrs Crupp's.

Commentary

There is something ominous at the opening of the chapter when we learn that Littimer is to remain behind in Yarmouth. Steerforth's account of Doctors' Commons is satirical, but he has an eye to the main chance, and believes that David will make money there. Betsey is as full as ever of her obsession about the donkeys; her essential goodness is always evident. She also reveals her generosity in paying for David to be articled. There are hints here of course of the existence of her husband. The incident is a melodramatic one but quickly over, and we contemplate the caricature of Mr Spenlow with his affectation and protection – the partner Mr Jorkins who is never if ever called upon to speak. Mrs Crupp, who is to play some part in David's life from now on, is also vividly drawn.

Doctors' Commons A society of lawyers, incorporated in 1768, in buildings near St Paul's Cathedral, with exclusive rights of dealing with Ecclesiastical, Admiralty and Probate cases. The proctors resembled solicitors in their functions. They were admitted to the society by fiat of the Archbishop. Dickens worked in Doctors' Commons from the age of seventeen. The charter of Doctors' Commons was not given up until 1857.

the days of the Edwards i.e. the Kings, the last being the boy Edward VI (1547–53).

plume Pride.

waiting supper i.e. having kept supper for herself and David.

here to my surprise she hesitated, and was confused Plot clue about her husband having claims upon her.

St Dunstan's At St Dunstan's in Fleet Street there was a famous clock which had a mechanism by which figures of boys struck the hours on bells with poleaxes. The church was pulled down in 1830, but the clock was set up again at Dunstan Villa in Regent's Park.

temple, accessible to pilgrims Note the irony.

an Arches day The ecclesiastical court of appeal of the Archbishop of Canterbury, so named because it was formerly held in the Church of St Mary-le-Bow, whose steeple was 'raised at the top with stone pillars in fashion like a bow bent archwise'.

the Consistory Court Under the jurisdiction of the Bishop including, until 1857, matrimonial and probate cases.

Prerogative Court The court where wills were proved, replaced by a new civil Probate court in 1858.

Admiralty Court The court which decided maritime cases both in peace and war.

Delegates' Court The Court of appeal until 1832 from the Ecclesiastical and Admiralty courts.

Mr Jorkins would have his bond A deliberately ironic echo of Shylock's determination to have his bond, i.e. Antonio's pound of flesh, in Shakespeare's *The Merchant of Venice*.

at little roadside inns of argument Fine image to indicate the meandering nature of the investigation.

the Adelphi Infinitely desirable area overlooking the Thames.

a sweet set they is for sich i.e. a good set of rooms they are for such a person.

summun Someone.

Chapter 24

David goes to Highgate but finds that Steerforth is not there. The next morning he receives a visit from his friend, and invites him with two of his (Steerforth's) friends to dinner that evening. David has too much to drink and afterwards they all go to the theatre, and there David in his drunken state sees Agnes, who wisely urges him to let his friends take him home. The next morning he is full of remorse and also has a hangover.

Commentary

The eccentricities of Mrs Crupp already begin to make themselves felt; she is both lazy and incapable of changing her way of life. The humour of their being dependent on the pastry-cook gives way to the humour of the meal itself, and the wonderful way that everything is seen through David's drunken haze. It is an insight into human error and self-exposure, with David taking too much snuff, smoking too much and for the first time anyway, talking to himself, all of this done with a fine running vivacity by Dickens. The slurred speech is accurately and convincingly evoked, becoming both embarrassing and humorous at the theatre as David tries to enunciate his surprise at seeing his mentor and, at this stage, unconsciously-loved Agnes. There is too a foreshortening of time, and the aftermath of a moral and physical hangover is upsettingly captured.

Dutch-oven A cheap portable oven.
'rather a tight fit' i.e. there was not enough of it.
'When the heart of a man is depressed with care' Another song from *The Beggar's Opera* – see note p. 38.
the Lares In ancient Rome the 'lares' were deified ancestors and with the 'penates' they made up the household gods. Here the word is synonymous with 'home' and all that it stands for.
Neverberrer Never better.
Lorblessmer! Lord bless me!

Revision questions on Chapters 13–24

1 Describe David's journey as he runs away from the Murdstones. In what way does it illustrate Dickens's narrative powers?

2 Bring out the humour and the drama in the meeting between Betsey Trotwood and the Murdstones.

3 Write a character sketch of Uriah Heep as he appears so far in these chapters.

4 Compare and contrast Mr Wickfield and Dr Strong, or Mr Dick and Mrs Markleham, or Rosa Dartle and Agnes.

5 Do you regard Steerforth as thoroughly selfish, or do you consider that he has a conscience? Support your answer by referring to the text.

6 Indicate the part played by the Micawbers and Tommy Traddles in this section.

7 What changes do you think have taken place in David's character during these chapters?

Chapter 25

David receives a note from Agnes asking him to come to Mr Waterbrook's, where she is staying. He goes there, and during the conversation she warns him against Steerforth. More significantly in a sense, she tells him that Uriah Heep has acquired considerable power over her father and that they are shortly to go into partnership. David goes to dinner at Mr Waterbrook's the next day, and there meets one of the favourites of his schooldays, Tommy Traddles. Going home, he invites Uriah Heep back to his lodgings; he learns from him of his changed relationship to Mr Wickfield. More importantly, and worst of all, he also learns that Uriah has ambitions to marry Agnes.

Commentary

This chapter gives evidence of Dickens's range. Notice to begin with Agnes's sensitivity and kindness in writing to David without mentioning the theatre incident. Her insight into Steerforth is disconcerting to David, but already it shows her almost motherly (David at this stage would say 'sisterly') concern for him. We also have to measure the moral courage it takes her to utter this; we suspect that she is in love with David. The presence of Heep and the prospective partnership is even more disconcerting. These personal revelations are admirably complemented by the satirical verve which marks the account of the dinner party, and there is a particularly neat touch in Mr Waterbrook's condescension over Tommy Traddles. There is also a sharp description of being too genteel and on 'Hamlet's aunt'. This superficial society is replaced in turn by the intimacy, be it ever so 'umble, of Uriah Heep. His ambitions with regard to Agnes revolt David and the reader, but we can't help noting David's blindness with regard to his own feelings for Agnes here. The range of the moral commentary in this chapter is remarkable, for the dinner party throws up the limpets of society, with their evaluations of 'blood' and money. It is a conscious anticipation of the description of the Veneerings in *Our Mutual Friend* (1864–6).

Titans Giants or monsters, from giants of ancient mythology.

Shakespeare has observed . . . 'an enemy into his mouth' is a slightly adapted quotation from *Othello* 2, 3, 280.

plunged into a vapour bath i.e. the smells of cooking.

Conscience made cowards of us both This time an adapted quotation from *Hamlet* 3, 1, 83.

all iced for the occasion A finely satirical way of describing social coldness and reserve.

Blood i.e. aristocratic descent.

Court Circular The name given after 1813 to the officer of the Court who had the responsibility for passing on to the newspapers the movements and any news concerning the Royal Family.

the family failing of indulging in soliloquy A neatly ironic twist – since Hamlet soliloquizes so much in the play, any aunt of his (here Mrs Spiker) might be expected to do the same.

beau ideal i.e. the highest type of excellence.

a great Guy Fawkes pair of gloves i.e. only fit for a guy to wear. But remember that Uriah is a plotter, hence the aptness here.

with the appropriately red light of the fire The suggestion is of the Devil.

ponyshay i.e. pony-chaise.

'I'd crown resigns . . . mine' A line from the refrain of the celebrated 'The Lass of Richmond Hill', a popular song by Leonard Macnally (1752–1820).

his mouth open like a post-office The vivid image virtually defines Heep's capacity for getting all the information he can.

Chapter 26

Mr Spenlow invites David to spend a weekend at his home so that they can celebrate his being articled to the firm. David gives an account of the way in which business is conducted in Doctors' Commons. He meets Dora, Mr Spenlow's daughter, and falls in love with her at first sight. He is somewhat taken aback when he finds she is virtually under the guardianship of a 'confidential friend', who turns out to be Miss Murdstone. Although they admit to knowing each other, she and David agree to pose as 'distant acquaintances'. When David returns home, because of his actions and reactions, Mrs Crupp sees that he has fallen in love.

Commentary

David continues to be full of foreboding on Agnes's account with regard to Heep. He also continues to be blind about the nature of his own feelings towards Agnes, or perhaps it is that these feelings are in abeyance anyway. Notice how selective David is about the passage of time (as a good writer should be – and David is to become a successful writer). Despite being articled, he is able to wax satirical about Doctors' Commons, though he is very much aware of the moral issues involved. The love-at-first-sight experience is qualified by the presence of Miss Murdstone. This is a master-stroke of the unexpected. David's immediate obsession with Dora does not extend to Jip, while Dora's treatment of her pet is an index to her own character – she is just as spoiled as he is, has been made just such a pet of. David now becomes even more of a romantic daydreamer than hitherto; his purchase of the waistcoats and his mooning about in the hope of seeing Dora are unconscious comedy too. From time to time, however, one gets the feeling that David is laughing at himself from his present standpoint, having the benefit of hindsight. His exchanges with Mrs Crupp are comedy in a broader, more obvious vein.

detestable Rufus From the Latin *rufus* = red, and hence the name given to people with red hair.
the spazzums i.e. spasms.
in fragments of English versification i.e. David wrote poetry.
The Stranger An adaptation and translation by Benjamin Thompson (1776–1816) of a play by the German dramatist Kotzebue (1761–1819). It was a success when first presented in England at Drury Lane in 1798, and was a Doctors' Commons play because it dealt with marital problems.
phaeton Light four-wheeled carriage.
East India sherry A very fine sherry which had matured in the East Indies.
Consistory See note p. 40.
pretty pickings i.e. good fees.
eulogium Extravagant praise.
had seen the cards shuffled ... played A satirical way of describing the lottery of Doctors' Commons.
life-preserver A truncheon reinforced with lead.
lackadaisical young spoony i.e. feebly sentimental and romantic.
by the board i.e. not been considered.
cardamums East India spice.
in some indistinct association ... David is being ironic. In fact it is a very distinct association with a 'copper' 'full' of washing.
the present set i.e. of rooms

Chapter 27

David visits Traddles in Camden Town. Arrived outside the house he finds there is an argument going on about the milk bill, which reminds him of the Micawbers. Traddles explains to David that he is reading for the bar (a plot hint here of Traddles's later activities against Heep), and describes how he supplements his poor income by hack writing. He also reveals that he is engaged to the daughter of a curate. David finds to his surprise that Traddles is in fact lodging with the Micawbers.

Commentary

Though David is loyal to Traddles, we note at once that he is somewhat snobbish about the neighbourhood – after all, he is moving in different circles now. The scene with the milkman contains another social comment on the penalties of poverty, but the Micawber associations of the scene are so redolent of the Micawber past (and future) that we are not really surprised to find that Traddles is their lodger. Traddles's character is self-evident – loyal, straightforward, somewhat simple (that is not a derogatory term), generous, and forgiving when it comes to the monstrous Creakle. Traddles fills in the gaps with his retrospect, and David is human enough to envy his being engaged. There is something decent and responsible about Traddles's attitude, but the reintroduction of the Micawbers immediately provides an accretion of narrative interest. Mr Micawber is still in good voice, Mrs Micawber eloquent too though again 'expecting'. Traddles, we feel, is now in David's former relationship with the family.

reading for the bar Studying at one of the inns of court to be a barrister.
a great pull i.e. a large inducement.
in statu quo (Lat.) I am as I was: my situation is unchanged.
the enjoyment of salubrity i.e. in good health
immortalized by Chaucer A reference to *The Canterbury Tales*, by Geoffrey Chaucer (1340–1400), the collection of tales in verse supposed to have been told by a party of pilgrims on their way to the shrine at Canterbury.
hard-bake sweets made of treacle, almonds, sugar and lemon-juice.
a Bow-street officer ... Policemen in the early nineteenth century were called Bow Street runners, because Bow Street was the site of the main London Police Court. Sir Robert Peel established the constabulary in 1828.

Chapter 28

David invites Traddles and the Micawbers to dine at his lodgings. In the middle of the festivities Littimer arrives to ask if Steerforth has been there. Mrs Micawber believes that Mr Micawber should contribute to the possibility of something turning up by advertising his qualifications in the newspapers. Just before they depart, Mr Micawber hands David a letter. They have hardly gone when Steerforth arrives. He has just come from Yarmouth, and brings David a letter from Peggotty which contains the news that Barkis is not expected to live much longer. David resolves to visit her, but agrees to defer that visit until after he has spent the next day at Steerforth's house. When Steerforth leaves, David reads Mr Micawber's letter, which says that his position is hopeless and that he cannot repay Traddles's loan.

Commentary

David continues lovelorn as he lives 'principally on Dora and coffee'. Again there is the humour in the dinner, not least arising from Mrs Crupp's refusal to do anything and the inadequacy of David's arrangements. The Micawbers move inevitably from a domestic quarrel to the happiness occasioned by punch, with Mrs Crupp as a sick background figure. There is a splendid improvization of cookery before another unexpected manifestation, namely the arrival of Littimer.

Mr Micawber's advertising is comic-grotesque, as is his language and Mrs Micawber's, but the involvement of the good-natured Traddles in their debts gives David cause for concern. Steerforth's arrival, with his news of Barkis's state, provides dramatic interest and moves the plot forward, since it is clear that Steerforth, by delaying David's visit a day, is making sure of accompanying him to Yarmouth. Mr Micawber's letter is, in a sense, the story of his life – the extremes of either being taken or the exhilaration of not being taken are the words and punctuation of his existence.

ampial Ample, complete.
dumb-waiter A stand or wagon holding dishes.
the Hymeneal altar Hymen was the god of marriage in Greek myth.
ribald Turncock i.e. a water-worker who had abused him.
We twa hae run . . . A few lines from 'Auld Lang Syne' (gowans = daisies).
Barclay and Perkins . . . Buxton Names of old-established brewery firms.
contumely Treating with contempt and reproach.

a Roman matron The Roman housewife was held in great honour as the mother of Roman citizens and the greatest influence on their training – consider Volumnia in Shakespeare's *Coriolanus*.
The Dashing White Serjeant* and *Little Tafflin A song by General Burgoyne (words) and music by H. R. Bishop. The second is a song from *The Three and the Deuce* (1795) a comedy by Prince Hoare.
Sybarite A self-indulgent person, named after Sybaris, a town on the gulf of Tarentum, whose inhabitants were noted for their idle luxury.
Bacchanal A follower of Bacchus, the god of wine in classical mythology.
an immortal Writer The reference is to a usage by Shakespeare.

Chapter 29

David goes on his visit to Steerforth, but is somewhat surprised by the behaviour of Rosa Dartle, who seems intent on spying on all he does. She questions him in such a way as to blame him for Steerforth's absence. David tells her that he knows nothing different about Steerforth. At the latter's request, Rosa Dartle sings, but afterwards spurns him. Next morning David leaves for Yarmouth.

Commentary

Again David waxes satirical about a case in Doctor's Commons. Notice the absence of Littimer, an ominous plot indication, and the interesting structural balance in Rosa's suspecting David's influence on Steerforth, a kind of black equivalent of Agnes's suspicions of Steerforth's influence on David. The quality of Rosa's conversation shows the twisted nature of her mind: she is scarred emotionally as well as physically. She uses sarcasm as a protective reflex. Steerforth's propitiation of her and her singing the unearthly song are two of the unpleasantly fascinating things in this chapter, as indeed are the two characters themselves. The chapter ends with sentiment, though we are moved by Steerforth's urging David to think of him at his best.

patrician Superior, the opposite of plebeian.
playing her harp The idea is associated with angels, hence the black humour here.

Chapter 30

David sees Mr Omer, who gives him the news that Em'ly is somewhat unsettled. Mr Omer says that Em'ly and Ham would have been man and wife by now but for Barkis's illness. When David goes to Peggotty's house he immediately notices Em'ly's curious behaviour. It is put down to her fear of Barkis's death. Barkis seems just to recognize David before he 'goes out with the tide'.

Commentary

This moving chapter has the mystery of Little Em'ly, her behaviour full of clues for the discerning reader. The essential goodness of the Yarmouth people is therefore seen in contrast to Steerforth and his behaviour later. Barkis's death, with its tribute to C. P. Barkis, is beautifully and, for Dickens, reticently done. The real focus is on Em'ly and her clinging to her uncle – and her deep fears.

engaged Made a reservation for, booked.
srub (Shrub): rum with lemon juice.
nailed down i.e. tied, but coming from Mr Omer it suggests the coffin.

Chapter 31

Barkis has hoarded successfully over the years, and so Peggotty is well provided for. When David visits Mr Peggotty he finds him in an illusory state of happiness, for shortly afterwards Ham arrives with a pathetic note from Em'ly to say that she has run away. It soon becomes clear that she has gone with Steerforth. Mr Peggotty determines to go and find her and bring her back wherever she might be.

Commentary

Despite the will and funeral of Barkis, the main concern of this chapter is the action of Em'ly. Attention focuses on the terrible effect on Ham, on David, and perhaps above all on Mr Peggotty. It is done with direct dramatic impact. Notice that these short chapters have the effect of moving the plot forward quickly.

A cloud is lowering on the distant town... Rather obvious use of symbol to indicate the news to come.
azackly Exactly.
visionary Strap See note on Chapter 4.
stave in Break up.

Chapter 32

David seeks out his friends, to learn that they have made their arrangements. These are that Mrs Gummidge will look after the house while Mr Peggotty travels in search of Em'ly. Miss Mowcher appears and gives David an account of Steerforth's treachery. David goes to London with Peggotty and Mr Peggotty. Mr Peggotty and David call on Mrs Steerforth, but get no satisfaction from her and learn nothing. Rosa responds passionately to the news of Steerforth's behaviour, and shows her jealousy, hatred and scorn of Em'ly in a singularly unfeeling way. Mr Peggotty then sets out on his long search.

Commentary

The opening of this chapter, with David's feelings still strong for Steerforth in his adversity, is beautifully registered from David's consciousness. His fear that Ham will kill Steerforth if he meets him shows how completely he is entering into the suffering of his friends. Notice the exquisite sensitivity of Mr Peggotty's leaving Mrs Gummidge in charge (p. 451) so that Em'ly might be persuaded to sneak back into her old home knowing that there is only a woman there. The crisis, the anguish, brings out the best in Mrs Gummidge, who now begins to think of others and not of herself. The chapter is full of miniature scenes, such as the child of Mrs Joram crying for Em'ly. Once more there is a dramatic unexpectedness about Miss Mowcher's arrival. Her attack on David's gullibility with regard to Steerforth is a sustained one, and she also reveals that she suspected that David himself was 'a young libertine'.

The encounter between Mr Peggotty and Mrs Steerforth is a moving one because of the quiet dignity of the man and the self-contained obduracy and pride of the woman. The class difference not only between these two but between Steerforth and Em'ly is given a very strong stress. Mrs Steerforth's outburst is a study in embittered selfishness. David's sensitivity gives him an insight into the interaction between mother and son, both proud and obstinate. But there is nothing to match the bitterness of Rosa Dartle in its vindictive and physical fury. The chapter ends with the determination of Mr Peggotty to see the search through in quietness and faith.

a mort i.e. a great deal.
kiender Kind of, sort of.

furder Further, more.
stan'ning Standing, being.

Chapter 33

David reminds the reader that throughout the happenings he was still in love with Dora. When he returns to work he proves Barkis's will. One day Mr Murdstone comes into the office to get a wedding licence. David discusses the Prerogative Office with Mr Spenlow, who then invites David down for Dora's birthday party. Completely infatuated, David visits Dora at the house of her friend Miss Mills. The picnic is described, David is often frustrated and jealous, but proposes to Dora and they become secretly engaged so that Dora's father does not know.

Commentary

This is a chapter of contrasts, the sombre side being provided by the reappearance of Mr Murdstone, about to make another profitable marriage. The interaction between him, David and Peggotty is indeed a bitter one. There is further satire on Doctors' Commons before Dora re-enters the action, with Jip much in evidence and Miss Mills understanding the affairs of the heart, with her own experience ever foremost. Notice that she in fact arranges the affair, David being invited to visit her after the picnic to make the proposal. We feel (a) that the secrecy will lead to trouble and (b) the sensitivity of David when he (from his position of author/narrator) refers to the ring on the finger of his daughter and its resemblance to that past ring of Dora's.

like a little lighthouse . . . stationery Note the image – almost an unconscious anticipation of the sea sequence to come.
some perspiring Waxwork There were many waxwork shows in London, though this could be a reference to Madame Tussaud's.
Miss Linwood's exhibition This consisted of representations in needlework of well-known pictures.
the Surrogate's The Surrogate was the Bishop's deputy. He had the power to take oaths for marriage licences.
Vicar-General's Office Office of the Archbishop's Chancellor or assistant in ecclesiastical cases.
cut up i.e. upset.
an ingenious little statute This refers to an Act of 1753 by which, as in this instance, the giving of a wrong name or the omission of a Christian

name at marriage constituted grounds for annulment. In 1823 this law was altered.
pluralist A clergyman holding more than one benefice.
three pun sivin i.e. Three pounds and seven shillings (the latter about 35 pence).
noodle Idiot.
might, could, would, or should A quotation from *Grammar of the English Language* (1795), by Lindley Murray, a very popular grammar book.
a Voice from the Cloister i.e. as one who had given up life to become a nun.
cocked-hat note A note folded into a shape resembling that of a cocked hat.

Chapter 34

David writes to Agnes about Dora. Later Traddles visits him and talks about his fiancée Sophy and the rest of her family. He also gives news of Mr Micawber, who has temporarily changed his name to Mortimer because of his creditors. Traddles has lost property to Micawber's brokers. But Peggotty comes to the rescue and buys the articles back. When David goes back to his apartments he finds Betsy Trotwood and Mr Dick waiting for him. His aunt tells him that she has lost all her property and that she is ruined.

Commentary

It is typical that David should confide in Agnes and ask her approbation, since he values her response more than anyone else's. There is much mention of money and domestic economics generally in this chapter, with the Micawbers' affairs rebounding on Traddles. The latter again reveals his decency and loyalty with regard to Sophy, and Peggotty shows her character in the help she gives him and her response to Betsey. The collapse of Betsey's fortune is unexpected, but she is direct and unselfpitying about it.

Familiar Familiar spirit.
contract Contact.
pitchers i.e. jugs of water.
an execution i.e. an order to seize goods.
a pull i.e. a wrench, causing suffering.
broker i.e. pawnbroker.
brile Boil.

Chapter 35

David has to explain to Mr Dick what ruin means. Peggotty offers financial help, and Betsey questions David about Dora. David, after having tried ineffectually to resign his articles and to recover his premium, meets Agnes and takes her to his rooms. There Betsey tells how she came to lose her money. Agnes suggests that David should work as Dr Strong's secretary, Dr Strong having retired and come to live in London. Mr Wickfield calls with Uriah Heep, who has now got his partnership with him; his complete control over Wickfield is noted.

Commentary

There is the pathos of David's confiding in Mr Dick and in Mr Dick's reaction. Already Betsey is bent on economy, as we see from her refusal of her usual bedtime drink. She is greatly moved by the loyalty shown by Peggotty (or 'Barkis', as she calls her), evident by her willingness to provide for David and Betsey out of her own money. Betsey expresses her opinion that David is somewhat blind over Dora. There is a superb dream sequence that penetrates David's subconscious and reveals his fears of what may happen. There is some comedy when David tries to cancel his articles and is referred to Jorkins – this time a live Jorkins who soon scuttles to the bank. Part of David's dream is almost confirmed when Agnes tells him that Uriah Heep is sleeping in his old room. Agnes reveals her fears when she says 'I hope that real love and truth are stronger in the end than any evil or misfortune in the world.' Agnes's other deep fear is of course that her father may be implicated in Betsey's losses. The scene involving Wickfield, Heep and David has its moments of pathos because of Wickfield's abject attitude. The chapter ends with the beggar muttering 'Blind!', an echo of Betsey's words to David about Dora and an accurate comment on his state, his blindness to Agnes's love for him and his deep-down love for her.

a very monument of human misery A clever use of the image most associated with Mr Dick to underline his reactions to events.

hucksters i.e. flower (and probably fruit) sellers.

'British Judy' i.e. a British Jury.

Tom Tiddler nonsense From the children's game of 'Tom Tiddler's ground' where money can be 'fished up easily'.

galvanic A word derived from its inventor Galvani, the implication here being that Heep is jerking about as if suffering electric shocks.
the red fox A reference to Heep's red hair.

Chapter 36

David goes to see Dr Strong and has the prospect of earning £70 a year for helping him compile his dictionary. He meets Mrs Strong and also Jack Maldon, who has returned from India. Traddles finds employment for Mr Dick and David decides to learn shorthand with a view to becoming a Parliamentary reporter. Traddles has a letter for David from Mr Micawber. David and Traddles visit Mr Micawber, who announces that he is going to remove with his family to Canterbury, since he is going to become a confidential clerk to Uriah Heep. Mr Micawber gives Traddles an IOU as an outward means of discharging his debts.

Commentary

David is full of ideals and enthusiasm (hence the chapter title) in his determination to work and thus win Dora. We note the generosity of Dr Strong, and his broad tolerance in finding something for Jack Maldon to do. Maldon is a study in boredom, and his languor gives David the opportunity to indulge in a little social satire. Ironically David, himself somewhat blind, feels Dr Strong's blindness to what he construes as his wife's preference for Jack Maldon. Meanwhile David inadvertently puts Mr Dick in the way of greater fulfilment by bringing him into Traddles's company and the latter, with typical kindness of heart, puts him in the way of copying documents. There is yet another entertaining and unpredictable coming together with the Micawbers. Mrs Micawber's ambitions for her husband's rise to an ultimate in elevation provides most of the running commentary of the chapter. There is too a theme of more serious import, perhaps best referred to in David's apprehensions with regard to Micawber's employment with Heep. This is an important plot point. Best of all is the conclusion of the chapter with Mr Micawber erect at the knowledge that he has paid his debts to Traddles – which of course he hasn't.

my woodman's axe Expressive image indicative of David's practicality.
a little Patent place i.e. as an agent to people who wished to take out patents.

There's an account about the people being hungry... There was a high level of unemployment and misery in the North, with the high price of bread before Peel's repeal of the Corn Laws in 1846 causing much distress. Note Maldon's contempt, a further indication of his moral debasement in his indifference to the sufferings of others.

from China to Peru Part of the second line of Dr Johnson's poem *The Vanity of Human Wishes* (1749).

it may be for years... for ever a quotation from the song 'Kathleen Mavourneen' by Julia Crawford (1800–85).

like the Phoenix The mythological bird which, after living for five hundred years, burnt itself to ashes on a funeral pile, from which a new Phoenix arose.

***Commentaries*... Mr Justice Blackstone** Sir William Blackstone (1723–80) was the first Vinerian Professor of English Law at Oxford. He became a judge in 1770, but is chiefly remembered for his *Commentaries on the Laws of England* (1765–69).

on the woolsack The seat of the Lord Chancellor in the House of Lords. It is a bag of wool covered with cloth, and was adopted in the reign of Edward III to emphasize to the Lords the wool trade's importance to England.

head-voice Voice capable of high notes.

The Wood-Pecker tapping A song by Thomas Moore (about 1820).

cognomen Additional name.

Revision questions on Chapters 25–36

1 Write an essay on David's falling in love and say how it affects his character.

2 Indicate the parts played by Traddles and the Micawbers in these chapters.

3 Write an essay on Dickens's use of contrast in these chapters (for example, on the theme of 'Loss').

4 Write a character study of any *three* characters whose lives have a considerable effect on David in these chapters.

5 Write a detailed appreciation of any one scene involving (a) pathos or (b) humour in these chapters.

Chapter 37

Betsey takes over David's domestic arrangements, and completely defeats Mrs Crupp. Peggotty returns to Yarmouth. David visits Dora at Miss Mills's and tells her of his changed prospects. She is quite unequal to the situation, but this in no way undermines David's infatuation with her.

Commentary

David deliberately drives himself hard – and there is little doubt that he enjoys driving himself hard. David's visit to Dora is prepared by Miss Mills with her comic signalling, but the high watermark of the chapter is unquestionably the putting down of Mrs Crupp by Betsey. This is rich comedy, with Mrs Crupp reduced to keeping out of the way. Peggotty's journey calls forth another generous gesture from her with regard to David. All that is spoiled in Dora – and it is almost completely all – responds to David's news. It reveals her incapacity for life. She is, as she says, frightened of practicality. David's power of decision, even the mention of the Cookery Book, frightens her even more; there is a simulated crisis, but David is unable to relinquish his love.

gramnivorous Grass eating.
darkly shadowed it forth i.e. prepared her for the change (of his now being poor).
a decanter-stand in his mouth i.e. here, for collecting money.
a navigator The word 'navvy' (labourer) is derived from it. Here the word means a 'digger of canals'.

Chapter 38

David learns shorthand and practises Parliamentary reporting with the help of Traddles; he also involves Mr Dick and Betsey in his training. But at the office David learns from Dora's father Mr Spenlow that Miss Murdstone, also present, has come across his letters to Dora. Mr Spenlow forbids any continuation of the affair, but later, during the evening of the same day, Mr Spenlow suddenly dies. He has left no will, and in fact it is revealed that he has very little to leave anyway. Dora goes to live with her aunt at Putney.

Commentary

Events move fast in this chapter. There is a brilliant comic focus on David's involving others in his training to be a reporter, which takes the arduousness off what he is doing. We feel David's suffering during the interview with Mr Spenlow and Miss Murdstone. There is a terrible irony in that part of the Spenlow lecture to David which deals with 'testamentary arrangements', while he himself has been unwise enough to make none of his own. There is also the irony that we feel he suspects David when in fact David cannot gain from what Mr Spenlow has not got. Even in his adversity, David realizes that Julia Mills is enjoying the situation. The suddenness of Mr Spenlow's death is dramatically effective, but there is a searing self-honesty about David that we are forced to admire, for he feels that he will be displaced from Dora's heart by her loss of her father. David's diary shows the record of his suffering and also dwells on the length of time involved. His diary entry is sentimental, melodramatic and self-indulgent, all that we should expect at this stage in his existence.

my tempest-driven bark a romantic way of describing his anguished attempts to learn short-hand.

Enfield's *Speaker* William Enfield (1741–97) was a Protestant clergyman who became famous for his religious views and for *The Speaker* (1774), an elocution book that remained popular for a long time.

Mr Pitt William Pitt (1759–1806). Son of the Earl of Chatham. He became Prime Minister in 1783 at the age of 24. He is famous as 'the pilot that weathered the storm' of the French Revolutionary Wars.

Charles James Fox (1749–1806) Famous orator and political opponent of Pitt.

Mr Sheridan Richard Brinsley Sheridan (1751–1816) the celebrated dramatist (author of *The Rivals* and *The School for Scandal*) who became a politican and supporter of Fox after 1780.

Mr Burke Edmund Burke (1729–97). Famous for his speeches on the question of American Independence and the French Revolution.

Lord Castlereagh (1769–1822) The Foreign Secretary who played a great part in the peace settlement after Waterloo (1815).

Viscount Sidmouth (1757–1844) The Tory politician who was Prime Minister 1801–04.

George Canning (1770–1827) The rival of Castlereagh. He was Foreign Secretary 1822–27.

the Dragon of Wantley The title of a comic 17th-century ballad telling of a dragon in Yorkshire which devoured cattle and children.

Evening Bells A song by Thomas Moore (1778–1852).

verses respecting self and young gazelle The verses referred to are in 'The Fire-Worshippers', the third verse tale in *Lalla Rookh* by Thomas Moore, the Irish poet. The idea is that whatever one loves is sure to die.

Patience on Monument 'Like Patience on a monument/Smiling at grief'. (Viola in Shakespeare's *Twelfth Night*, Act 2, Scene 4,116.)

Chapter 39

David pretends that he should go to Dover to attend to his aunt's affairs, but in reality he is concerned about Agnes and makes this the excuse for calling at Canterbury on the way back. There he finds Mr Micawber working for the partnership, but he is uneasy and reticent about his work. Agnes advises David to write to Dora's aunts so that he can have access to her, while Uriah Heep suspects that David is his rival for Agnes. Heep, with his mother constantly in attendance, tells David of the charity school origin of his 'umbleness'. There is an unpleasant after-dinner scene when Wickfield breaks down at the thought of Heep becoming Agnes's husband. He bitterly bewails his present position. Afterwards, Heep still insists that he will have Agnes.

Commentary

David's dejection, followed by a swingeing attack on the system of inveigling, that is, touting for custom at Doctors' Commons. The visit to Canterbury is both dramatic and functional to the plot, with Mr Micawber's attitude – and his being bound to Heep – most significant. Heep's uneasiness is seen in his putting David in his place. David is profoundly moved in his interview with Agnes, an indication of how deeply his feelings are running with regard to her. Her advice to him is practical and full of reassurance, typical of her consideration for him, her determined ability to put her own feelings down. David is also taken in an unpleasant way with the 'umbleness' of Mrs Heep and the evil that she too generates. Her knitting has a menacing and mechanistic quality about it. In a superb image Dickens refers to the Heeps as being 'like two great bats hanging over the whole house'. David's attacks on Uriah have little or no effect. Heep's account of his father is almost a psychological explanation of himself. The dinner and after-dinner scene is high drama. Heep's cunning is seen in his playing on Mr Wickfield's weakness over drink, but Wickfield's grief and abject recognition of what he has done to himself is poignant revelation, for, as he puts it, 'I have preyed on my own morbid coward heart'. Agnes's own grief is understandable, and David unconsciously injures her with his 'Think of the priceless gift of such a heart as yours, of such a love as yours!'

Jack Ketch The 17th-century public hangman who executed the Duke of Monmouth in 1685.

a foundation school A school that is endowed and which therefore does not require fees.

Chapter 40

The letter to Dora's guardian aunts is posted. On returning home one night David meets Mr Peggotty on the steps of St Martin's church. He tells David how he has searched for Em'ly through France, Italy and Switzerland, showing David a letter which Em'ly has written and which was received by Mrs Gummidge. In the letter was five pounds. He tells David that he is about to leave for a town on the Upper Rhine where Em'ly's letter was post-marked. All this is overheard by Martha Endell, the girl Em'ly had once helped.

Commentary

Notice the affection between David and Betsey at the beginning of this chapter, which contrasts so effectively with what has just passed. The sight of Martha Endell provides drama, and the whole of the exchange with Mr Peggotty shows the latter's determination, love and nostalgia. He is, of course, both surrogate father and grandfather to Em'ly. He shows a remarkable degree of intuition with regard to Em'ly's travels and where she was likely to go, as well as an incredible degree of stamina. Em'ly's letter is moving but makes for sentiment and melodrama rather than realism. At the end of the chapter the snow is used symbolically to underline the purity, honesty, innocence of Mr Peggotty.

thowts . . . inquiration Thoughts . . . inquiries.
fust . . . sech First . . . such.

Chapter 41

The aunts invite David to meet them. He goes, accompanied by Traddles, who first of all tells him of his experiences with his fiancée's family. Conditions laid down by the aunts permit David to visit Dora at Putney, and as a result of this Betsey and the Misses Spenlow meet for the first time. David is rather troubled by the fact that everybody seems to regard Dora as a pretty toy; though she herself accepts this character, David continues unabatedly in love with her.

Commentary

There is light comedy about the exchange of correspondence and the tone of Dora's aunts, also about Miss Mills's departure for India. There is further humour about Traddles's hair, also about his courtship of Sophy, but this is surpassed by the formality of David's reception by the aunts. There is a delightful emphasis on Miss Lavinia's being an expert on affairs of the heart, and an equally delightful focus on the proprietary exchanges between the two ladies. Their performance is a set piece of positional interaction. Their laying down of the terms of David's visits to Dora has its own prepared formality. Dora is as spoiled as ever, prejudiced against Traddles and Miss Betsey before she meets her. It is quite typical of David to write to Agnes once he is admitted to Dora's company, and typical too of Dora to suffer a headache at the merest contemplation of the cookery book. Her reactions at this stage bode ill for the future.

suit of bills i.e. handbills advertising the contents for sale.
a fretful porcupine The quotation is from *Hamlet*, Act 1, Scene 5, line 20.
Bath water The medicinal mineral water of Bath, the famous spa.
with a damask rose . . . preyed upon Another half quotation, this time from *Twelfth Night*, Act 2, Scene 4.
an excellent kind of girl for Traddles There are times when David is condescending – Sophy turns out to be much more capable than Dora.

Chapter 42

Wickfield and Agnes pay a visit to Dr Strong. Naturally they are followed by Uriah Heep, who throws out hints to David that there is a love relationship between Jack Maldon and Mrs Strong. David takes Agnes to Putney to meet Dora. When he returns he goes to say goodnight to Dr Strong and finds Heep and Wickfield already there. Heep has revealed to the doctor his suspicions of the affair between Jack Maldon and his wife. Dr Strong refuses to cast any aspersions on his wife's honour, and blames himself for any unhappiness she may have suffered or be suffering. David, exasperated, strikes Heep for dragging his name into it. Mr Dick becomes a sympathetic link between the Doctor and Mrs Strong. Meanwhile David receives a letter from Mrs Micawber, informing him of the present secrecy and moroseness of her husband. She has turned to David for advice.

Commentary

The opening of this chapter with its 'even though this manuscript is intended for no eyes but mine' has a strongly autobiographical flavour without complacency about the narrator's talent and hard work. Heep is cunning as usual, though in fact he has echoed David's deepest suspicions of Jack Maldon and Mrs Strong. The meeting between Dora and Agnes carries overtones of Dora's recognition of Agnes's worth – and with great sensitivity, of the fact that David ought to have loved Agnes instead. The latter reassures David by saying that she will never take the step that he dreads. In the company of Dr Strong Uriah now turns officious. Wickfield's abject weakness is all too apparent, but this is the first time that we have seen Uriah so arrogant. Dr Strong displays humanity, dignity and compassion. He also shows his very real understanding of the differences between himself and his wife, and generously takes on his own shoulders what blame he feels there is. David's action in striking Heep is the result of extreme provocation, since he knows, to use his own words, that Uriah has set a trap for him in order to involve him in the supposed revelations to Dr Strong. Mr Dick is the humanizing influence that is to bring husband and wife together. Mrs Micawber's letter gives the chapter a perfect close.

a great East-India man i.e. a ship carrying goods to or from the East Indies.
guava An acid fruit used for making jelly, from the tropical tree of that name.
the man in the south This and the succeeding references are from an old nursery rhyme printed in *Songs from the Nursery* (1805).

Chapter 43

David takes up the story at the point where he is twenty-one years' old. He is still at Doctors' Commons, but at the same time is increasing his earnings by working as a Parliamentary shorthand reporter. This work is published in a morning newspaper, and he is also writing articles for magazines. His marriage to Dora is described.

Commentary

Again the autobiographical flavour will be noticed. The irony about Parliamentary debate and decision is marked. The successful writing is sufficient testimony to David's incredible industry (which is in turn testimony to his creator's). The retrospective narrative – done graphically in the present tense – captures the preparations for and mood of the marriage. There is a great deal of sentiment, with Betsey Trotwood, Dora and David himself playing leading parts in the action. The major stylistic device of the chapter is a series of paragraphs beginning with 'Of' to indicate the nature of the many happenings. At the end of the chapter 'the phantoms of those days' are gone and we prepare for the practicality of marriage.

savage stenographic mystery i.e. system of shorthand.
Britannia i.e. Great Britain, always mentioned in the Parliamentary debates.
to fee i.e. pay.
I wrote a little something This is very close to Dickens's own account of the posting of his first story in real life.
the third finger, and take in the fourth i.e. he is earning £350 pounds per annum.
Chinese house i.e. a small model.
the Stamp Office A stamp of a certain value is payable before a document becomes law: it is affixed to the document.
Jip's Pagoda Jip's Chinese (more correctly, Burmese) house.
always clasping Agnes by the hand i.e. because completely dependent on her to get through the ceremony.

Chapter 44

David and Dora are settled in their own small house, but they experience the difficulties of housekeeping. These difficulties lead to their first disagreement. Betsey shows a great deal of tact when she is asked by David to give Dora some practical advice. There are difficulties with the servants, and the young couple have a visit from Traddles. Dora asks David to think of her as his child-wife, since she is completely helpless in practical matters.

Commentary

There is a wonderfully humorous account of 'Paragon' and how she nearly undermines the lives of her employers, here David and Dora. Dora is inept, incapable of taking housewifely responsibility, with the result that David has to take more than his share of it and also to blame himself for the small domestic differences between them. David's own word to describe his wife after he has wounded her is that she is 'pathetic', and we might employ the same word too but with its modern connotation of 'inadequate'. David's exchange with Betsey shows that wise woman seeing into the heart of the matter, which, quite simply, is that David has married a woman in his mother's image. Betsey conveys a fine sense of tolerance gained as a result of experience. David appreciates the generosity of feeling that deters Betsey from interfering. David's own lack of experience – and of course Dora's – is completely exposed by the cheating servants. The dinner for Traddles reflects David's dissatisfaction with their lack of room, the comedy of the oysters further shows Dora's incompetence, but there is a genuine pathos which attends her efforts. David has a natural refuge in his additional work. He settles, with sentiment, for a child-wife and make-believe housekeeping.

a written character i.e. testimonial.
shell-jacket Short jacket which reaches to the waist at the back.
Excise returns i.e. records of how much had been sold.
discussed Drank, sat over.
shrub See note on 'srub' p. 48.

Chapter 45

There is a description of Mrs Markleham's relations with Dr Strong and her daughter. Mr Dick calls on David, has some idea of the situation with the Strongs, and determines to set things right. One evening at the doctor's Mrs Markleham observes that she has just seen him making his will. Mr Dick is left alone with Mrs Strong for a moment. Next she goes into her husband's study and tells him before everybody of the false position she has been placed in by the infamy of Jack Maldon. She tells him that her love for him is firm and unchanging. David finds himself pondering on one of the phrases that Mrs Strong has used.

Commentary

Mrs Markleham unwisely encourages Dr Strong's wish that her daughter should be entertained. As David says, 'she probed the doctor's wound without knowing it'. She enjoys much pleasure on Annie's account. Betsey is as ever right, and sees the effect of the Old Soldier's interference. The role of Mr Dick, in which he acknowledges his simplicity, is made crucial, so much so that we are inclined to think his simplicity is worth more than cleverness. It is also moving, for he is saving his copying-money for Betsey since she has saved him from being shut up. The announcement of Strong's making his will is dramatic; it shows his exquisite sensitivity, determined to do for his wife in death what he feels he has failed to do in life. Mrs Markleham reveals her insensitivity in her wordy narration. Annie's confession and retrospect is moving but given at too great a length to be convincing. The sentence that causes David so much concern – obviously because it reflects his own situation – is 'There can be no disparity in marriage like unsuitability of mind and purpose.' Annie's confession of love for her husband – father (note the balance with child-wife) is too surprisingly fluent to be true.

and a rubber i.e. of whist.
Dr Johnson The leading literary figure of the 18th century and compiler of the first great English Dictionary (1755).
it's making i.e. being compiled.
An Italian iron A rounded iron used for pressing lace.
give 'em to the chimney-sweepers for May-day i.e. when they took their traditional holiday.
Marplot A person who spoils something which might otherwise turn out well, from the name of the hero of a play called *The Busie Body* (1709) written by Mrs Centlivre (1667–1723).
Saint Alphage The Church of that name. St Alphage was Archbishop of Canterbury 1006–12. He was martyred by the Danish invaders in 1012.
my love was founded on a rock See Matthew, 7,24 and Luke, 6,48.

Chapter 46

About a year after his marriage David passes Mrs Steerforth's house. A servant girl comes out and asks him to step in and speak to Rosa Dartle. She calls Littimer, who gives an account of what has happened to Emily and Steerforth. The latter has deserted Em'ly, who has fled. Her whereabouts are not known, but Steerforth is still abroad. Rosa tells David why she and Mrs Steerforth wished him to know of this. David then seeks out Mr Peggotty who is often in London. David suggests, after he has given him the news, that they contact Martha, who is more likely than anyone else to know if Em'ly has come to London. They see Martha near Blackfriars Bridge and follow her.

Commentary

A strong autobiographical flavour about the opening, which registers the success of David as a writer. Rosa's cruelty and wishing evil upon Emily is frightful to behold. David at the same time notices that, though wicked, she is alluring. Littimer is admirably composed during his recital. What is singularly unpleasant is Steerforth's bequeathing Emily to Littimer, and the distraction this engenders in Emily. We also note that Littimer has been paid by Rosa Dartle to tell everything. David realizes the distance between himself and Mrs Steerforth in terms of their appreciation of the situation – particularly the misrepresentation of Emily that she and Rosa wilfully undertake. The meeting with Mr Peggotty is imbued with pathos.

snew Snowed.
arrize i.e. come to any conclusion.
I wouldn't fare to i.e. I wouldn't like to set him thinking about it.
fleet water i.e. not deep.

Chapter 47

Martha goes to a deserted spot on the banks of the river, clearly intending to commit suicide. David forestalls her and Mr Peggotty, reassuring her that she is in no way responsible for Emily's elopement with Steerforth, asks for her assistance in finding her niece should she be in London. When he returns home David sees a man in Betsey Trotwood's cottage garden. Betsey gives the man money to go away, then reveals her secret: he is her husband.

Commentary

The chapter opens with a superb description of the run-down neighbourhood through which they follow Martha. The rescue is melodramatic but good narrative tension. Martha is herself a character from melodrama rather than real life, the archtypal fallen woman of the Victorian period. Her language is conventionally middle- rather than working-class. Mr Peggotty demonstrates a full faith in human nature in trusting Martha. The latter's rejection of money rings false, but Dickens is intent on the moral point. We move from one melodramatic scene to another with Betsey's confrontation with her husband and her confession to David. On the whole, this chapter is not up to Dickens' usual high standard.

the great blank Prison This is Millbank prison.
the Great Plague The epidemic of bubonic plague in London in 1665 which caused the deaths of 68,000 people and necessitated mass burials.
told Counted out.

Chapter 48

David has now become a successful author and gives up his Parliamentary reporting. The domestic mismanagement continues unabated, and there are the particular misdemeanours of a page to make things worse. David does his best to form Dora's mind but it is already formed. He has a number of misgivings but takes the resolution to go on loving her as his child-wife. Her baby dies shortly after birth: Dora remains weak and is now virtually an invalid.

Commentary

The autobiographical flavour once more evident, since David, like Dickens, has achieved literary fame. There are some fine stylistic turns in this chapter, perhaps the best being the satirical reference to 'the music of the parliamentary bagpipes'. The description of the page and his subsequent arrest is laced with typical Dickensian humour. But the exchanges between David and Dora are serious, with Dora possessing a wilful capacity of misunderstanding what is being said. She always has recourse to tears, which are the standard reflex of emotional blackmail. But Dora too knows herself and almost hints that David would have done better to have married Agnes; still, she gets her own way. David is aware that, though he is happy, it is not the kind of happiness he had wanted. He repeats to himself often another telling phrase of Annie Strong's – 'The first mistaken impulse of an undisciplined heart'. The blossom image at the end of the chapter is a deliberate forecast of Dora's coming death.

Whittington ... Lord Mayor Dick Whittington in the story ran away because of ill-treatment, but returned when he thought he heard Bow bells ringing 'Turn again, Whittington, Lord Mayor of London'. There was in fact a real Richard Whittington who was Lord Mayor of London at the turn of the fourteenth century.
like scarlet-beans very quickly – 'runner' beans.
four and sixpence i.e. 22½ pence in today's money, but of course worth much more at that time.
touching a hamper i.e. about the food.

suborned Bribed.
intelligence News.
how the blossom withered in its bloom A direct anticipation of Dora's death.

Revision questions on Chapters 37–48

1 Write an account of the changes that occur in David's life after Mr Spenlow's death.

2 Which do you consider the funniest episode in these chapters, and why?

3 Compare and contrast Uriah Heep and Mr Wickfield.

4 Write a description of the domestic life of David and Dora, referring to specific incidents to bring out the nature of each character.

5 Compare and contrast Mrs Markleham and Betsey Trotwood.

6 Write an account of either (a) the scene in which Annie Strong reveals her feelings to her husband and the company or (b) the scene involving Martha Endell. Do you consider that either of these scenes makes a contribution to the novel?

Chapter 49

David receives a morbid letter from Mr Micawber asking him in a roundabout way to bring Traddles and meet him outside the King's Bench Prison. At the same time Traddles receives a letter from Mrs Micawber, which gives some account of her husband's unnatural behaviour. She implores Traddles to reason with Mr Micawber who, she has every suspicion, is coming to London. They meet Mr Micawber and take him to Miss Trotwood's house. There he is very impressed by the friendly behaviour of Mr Dick, but he is obviously so worn down by his troubles that he can't even make his favourite punch. Suddenly he bursts out in condemnation of his employer Uriah Heep, and afterwards asks them all to meet him at Canterbury that day week, where he will expose the 'intolerable ruffian – HEEP!'

Commentary

Mr Micawber's letter is full of his own flamboyant language – at times extreme and at others full of cliché ('The cup is bitter to the brim'). It gives direct cause for concern since Micawber reveals that he has not told his wife what he is doing. Structurally this letter runs parallel with Mrs Micawber's and maintains the narrative excitement. The meeting with Micawber contains the humour usually associated with him, but it also has a strong moral tone – its indictment of Heep is accompanied by strong praise for Agnes, and the tension is seen in Micawber's limited ability to control himself. He wants to reveal, does not want to reveal, but we note his affectionate and warm response to Mr Dick. The crisis arrives with Mr Micawber's dislocated but unconsciously funny actions, and his suppression and release is conveyed through a fine stylistic use of dashes and staccato phrases proceeding from his passion. It is fitting that he has the last word in yet another letter.

muniments Title deeds.
inditing Composing, writing.
D.V. *Deo Volente* (Lat.), God willing, all being well.
lemon-stunners Sweets rather like acid-drops.
the D The Devil.
d,o,n, i.e. the end of 'London'.
in esse . . . in posse (Lat.) who actually is . . . who may be.
our coarse national sports i.e. boxing.
mountebank . . . playing the barrel-organ i.e. the implication is that the Micawbers will be reduced to street entertainment and begging.
Immortal exciseman The Scots poet Robert Burns (1759–96) whose song 'Auld Lang Syne' they sang at Canterbury.
Each in his narrow cell . . . hamlet sleep A quotation from the famous *Elegy Written in a Country Churchyard* by Thomas Gray (1716–1771).

Chapter 50

Having left a message for Mr Peggotty, who is out, Martha Endell comes for David urgently and takes him to her room. As they ascend the stairs they see Rosa Dartle enter the room. From the adjoining garret they see the bitter interview between Rosa and Em'ly. David does not thrust himself forward, for he feels that Mr Peggotty should be the one to reclaim Emily. Just as Rosa Dartle leaves Mr Peggotty arrives, and Emily collapses into his arms.

Commentary

We marvel at Mr Peggotty's stamina as his journeys are revealed, and we also admire his optimism and faith. The meeting with Martha is somewhat melodramatic; it is what we have come to expect from this particular section of the plot. Again, the sordidness of the location is stressed as David and Martha enter the building where Em'ly is. Rosa Dartle is ahead of them on the staircase. Rosa's insane hatred of Em'ly is evident. Em'ly cannot defend herself against Rosa's vicious sadism. We wonder at David's holding back, but he is waiting for Mr Peggotty's arrival to rescue his beloved Em'ly.

raise the very stones against you An echo of Shakespeare's *Julius Caesar*, Act 3, Scene 2, line 233.
vendible i.e. goods for sale.

Chapter 51

Mr Peggotty recounts the story of Emily after she has been deserted by Steerforth. She has been ill, and eventually has come to London, where she has been helped by Martha. Mr Peggotty has formed the determination to take Emily to Australia and there begin a new life with her. He is also going to send Steerforth's money back to him. David goes with Mr Peggotty to Yarmouth. There he finds Mr Omer confined to a wheelchair but still cheerful. He is anxious to help Martha. Ham asks David to tell Emily of his feelings provided that this causes her no additional pain, and also to express his gratitude to Mr Peggotty. Mrs Gummidge is determined to accompany Mr Peggotty and Emily wherever they may go.

Commentary

Betsey shows her commonsense and Mr Peggotty his appreciation of her. With the eye of his imagination, Mr Peggotty sees all that has happened to Emily. She has met with kindness and charitable help abroad, but back at home she is on the brink of prostitution when she is saved by Martha. Mr Peggotty's decision is a brave one; he is conscious, as ever, not of himself but of Emily. He is the idealized good man, even planning to make provision for Mrs Gummidge. Mr Omer's reaction to being incapacitated also shows courage; he displays a generosity of spirit with regard to Emily, and gives Ham much praise for talking and reading to him in the evenings – 'All his life's a kindness.' Ham's confiding to David is deeply moving – he puts Emily's feelings before his own, and shows a noble insight that belies his humble (not Heep-like humble) birth. Mrs Gummidge too comes out of herself – the sufferings of those who have so helped her have made her push her own low and lorn feelings into the background. The sincerity of Ham and Mrs Gummidge brings this chapter alive – goodness is seen as being brought out by anguish and despair.

pervising ... clicketten providing ... idle chattering.
wownd wound.
Sermuchser So much so.
wheer neither moth nor rust Matthew, 6,19.
what it's the price on i.e. what has been paid.
furder Farther.
take the fat with the lean i.e. the good with the bad.
Siamese breed The King of Siam's proudest title was 'King of the White Elephant'. White elephants are rare (they are albinos) and have been worshipped as incarnations of Buddha.
wheer the wicked cease from troubling Job, 3,17.

Chapter 52

David and Traddles, accompanied by Betsey and Mr Dick, go to Canterbury to keep their appointment with Mr Micawber. At the inn he asks them to come to the office of Wickfield and Heep. There he indicts Heep, reading out his accusations and accompanying proofs of Heep's frauds and forgery in his dealings with Mr Wickfield. Betsey now gives the real reason for her quiet acceptance of her family losses. Traddles demands from Heep a deed of relinquishment as well as all the firm's books and papers. He tells him he must stay in his room until everything has been examined. Heep is forced to comply, the alternative being that he would be conducted to Maidstone Jail. Betsey, David and Mr Dick witness the reconciliation of Mr Micawber and his family now that he has released all his suppressed indignation. Betsey suggests that he might do well to emigrate to Australia, and offers him a loan to enable him to do so.

Commentary

This superb chapter has the wonderful scene of the humiliation of Heep. Before that Dora has the (for her) temerity to tease Betsey, but she is in reality unselfishly covering her own suffering in her illness. David indulges his nostalgia in Canterbury. Micawber has been sensible enough to consult Traddles prior to his revelations. There is a kind of formality in the way Mr Micawber sets up the scene. It opens with Uriah's slime, moves quickly to the Micawber denunciation, and Traddles, who is really the Master of Ceremonies, produces Mrs Heep as an addition to Uriah's humiliation. David realizes just what a consummate hypocrite Heep has been when he sees him drop his mask. Micawber's rhetoric is brilliantly sustained, his own courage unquestionable since by exposing Heep he leaves himself open to imprisonment for his own debts. The situation has a rich comedy as Micawber becomes physically (though ineffectually) aggressive. Also ineffectual is Mrs Heep, though her Ury does eventually come to terms. The contrast at the end of the chapter is markedly effective, with Mr Micawber entering the realms of imagination after having performed so successfully for the needs of fact.

playing Booty with my clerk i.e. playing deceitfully, even losing at first in order to win dishonestly later.
our lively neighbour the Gaul i.e. the Frenchman, who would call an office a 'bureau'.
cupidity greed.
to dwindle, peak, and pine A quotation from Shakespeare's *Macbeth*, Act I, Scene 3, line 23.
philosophic Dane ... worse remains behind The quotation is from *Hamlet*, Act III, Scene 4, line 179, the reference being to Hamlet's own philosophizing soliloquies.
deponents i.e. those making a deposition on oath.
Canterbury Pilgrimage the reference is to Chaucer's *The Canterbury Tales*.
For England, home, and beauty A quotation from the song 'The Death of Nelson' in the opera *The Americans* (1811) by John Braham (1774?–1856).
the venerable Pile Canterbury Cathedral.

Chapter 53

Time passes. Dora grows weaker, and one evening she asks David to send for Agnes. She also tells him that she believes she has been much too child-like for him and that she was never really fitted to be his wife. When Agnes arrives Dora makes it clear that she wishes to speak to her alone. David asks Agnes to go up to her. Dora dies; at the same time Jip dies too.

Commentary

This retrospect brings out David's acute suffering at the time, and his selective choice of episodes significantly shows that Dora is in fact braver in her adversity than she has been when in full life, if the phrase is not too strong. Dora even contributes to the make-believe that she will recover. The death of Jip and Dora at the same time is contrived, of course, but the death scene is made the more poignant by not being protracted – a further indication of how far Dickens has progressed in terms of his putting away sentiment since his previous novel, *Dombey and Son*, and the treatment there of little Paul's death.

Chapter 54

David decides to go abroad after the death of Dora in the hope that he will recover. Before doing so, however, he visits Canterbury in order to conclude the Heep business. There is some description of the Micawber emigration. Traddles has the good news that Mr Wickfield is both solvent and improving in health. He is also innocent, as we might have suspected, of making away with Betsey's money, which has been recovered from Heep, who has himself gone to London. It is agreed to pay off Mr Micawber's IOUs to Heep, and likewise to provide him with the money for the passage and a small amount of capital. When she and David are together in London, Betsey reveals what has been on her mind, and they witness the funeral of her husband. A letter from Mr Micawber begins with gloom and ends with rapture.

Commentary

There is some indication of the future relationship of David and Agnes despite David's grief. Mr Micawber is as comically verbose as ever in arranging things with Miss Trotwood – he has also arranged his family's preparations for their new life. Mrs Micawber's insight into her family's rejection of Mr Micawber in the past shows her sensitive nature with regard to what her husband would call pecuniary arrangements. We are made constantly aware of Betsey's silent suffering during the exchanges with Traddles. Mr Dick continues his good offices, now with Mr Wickfield. Agnes, as we should expect, reveals that she wishes to devote herself to her father. Betsey reveals that she has had some capacity for intrigue and good sense by keeping money by her, and also that she has burnt Wickfield's confession that he has robbed her. This is evidence of her nobility of nature. She is greatly borne down the next day, though, when she takes David to the hospital and he sees the plain hearse. Micawber's letter is typical – he always swings from one extreme to another.

our Boat is on the shore . . . the sea An adapted quotation from a poem by Lord Byron (1788–1824).
enthralled i.e. imprisoned.
incubus i.e. a threat hanging over him.
Consols = consolidated annuities – Government stock bearing an interest rate of 3 per cent.
Now's the day . . . slavery From Robert Burns' song 'Bannockburn, Robert Bruce's address to his army.'

Chapter 55

Peggotty tells David how Ham has taken leave of her and Mr Peggotty. David writes his emotionally tactful letter to Emily, receives a reply and resolves to take this down to Ham in Yarmouth. While he is on the way, a terrible wind gets up, and at Yarmouth itself there is a monstrous storm at sea. David learns that Ham is away at Lowestoft, but is expected to return the next day. The storm reaches new heights, and the next morning David goes down to the shore. There he sees a wrecked schooner close by. The men, of whom one seems particularly active, are swept into the sea, but the active one and three others manage to cling to the remaining mast. Ham arrives and determines to go into the sea to save the one remaining man – the active one – but he is battered by a mountainous wave. He gets to the wreck, but is hauled in dead. The body of the man he had tried to save is washed ashore. It turns out to be Steerforth's.

Commentary

The pathos of the opening gives way to the frenzied activity of the storm. David's concern for Ham shows his inherent nobility of nature. The description of the storm is one of the highlights of the novel – vivid, frightening, absolutely immediate as if we were there. There is a strong sense of the expectation of people nearby, and thus a continuing feeling of tension and apprehension. That tension is increased by the bringing in of news of sinkings. Everything is geared towards the climax. David's own excitement is almost intolerable to him and to the reader. The style reflects his mental and emotional activity in a number of short staccato sentences. The particularity with which the wreck is described shows Dickens sparing no important detail. Ham is not so much idealized as realized as he contemplates the sea and the wreck 'with the silence of suspended breath behind him'. The two deaths, like those previous two deaths of Dora and Jip, are done with splendidly effective economy, even to the point of Steerforth's being given no name.

If tan't, I'll bide it i.e. if my time hasn't come, I'll wait for it.

Chapter 56

David takes Steerforth's body to London, then calls on Mrs Steerforth to tell her of her son's death. Rosa Dartle passionately reproaches Mrs Steerforth and avows her past love for Steerforth. Mrs Steerforth is bowed down by grief. Steerforth's body is taken into the house.

Commentary

Again note the fine economy of the narrative. David is forced by his sensitivity to the atmosphere to lead up to the news of Steerforth's death; he is further moved by the fact of Mrs Steerforth's likeness to her dead son. Searingly dramatic is Rosa Dartle's attack on Mrs Steerforth. David tries to restrain her out of compassion for Mrs Steerforth. But Rosa takes a sadistic pleasure in demonstrating now that Steerforth is dead that he has in any case been mutilated by his mother's self-indulgence. There is truth in this, and truth too in her assertion that Steerforth had turned her into his doll. But her outburst is in reality a terrible self-indictment, for she is demoniac in her denunciations.

Chapter 57

David confides in Mr Micawber about Ham, and they decide that Mr Peggotty shall not know of his fate. Micawber's preparations for the voyage are described, as well as his final making of punch. No one from Mrs Micawber's family turns up, but David and Peggotty go on board at Greenwich to take leave of the emigrants. Mr Peggotty has decided not only to take Emily and Mrs Gummidge but Martha Endell as well.

Commentary

There is the usual distinctive humour as Mr Micawber's get-up is described and also in yet another near arrest from the Heep v Micawber pursuit. After his rescue Mr Micawber waxes lyrically poetic at the prospect of the voyage. The farewell has tinctures of sadness, but we take final leave of Emily. Peggotty is greatly moved.

the coffers of Britannia i.e. English banks.
Albion England.
Ostade Adrian Ostade (1610–85), a Dutch painter. His subjects include stables, interiors of hovels and inns, with a strong emphasis on the sordid and the squalid.

Chapter 58

Feeling that he has lost everything, David eventually settles in Switzerland. He is somewhat fortified by a letter from Agnes. He takes up his writing again and learns from passing travellers of his growing reputation. He comes to the full realization of his love for Agnes but feels that he cannot make her his own because he is afraid to disturb the relationship that has existed for so long between them. After a three years' absence he returns to England.

Commentary

The tracing of David's feelings is finely done from inside his consciousness. In fact it is a study in what we call depression. The accompaniment is silence and space, out of which thoughts gradually clarify. Nature speaks to him, and he breaks down and weeps. Agnes's letter becomes the source of David's strength and faith. He communes with Nature but he also communes with his work. He has listened to Dora's words in the past and now relates them to his lonely present. The Dickens autobiographical element with regard to David's writing is markedly present.

Chapter 59

When he reaches London David seeks out Traddles at Gray's Inn. His old school friend is now happily married to his Sophy, and five of her sisters are staying with them. David stays at the Gray's Inn Coffee House where he meets the doctor who delivered him, Mr Chillip. The doctor tells David that he is now living near Bury St Edmunds and that among his neighbours are the Murdstones. Mr Murdstone, with the help of his sister, has driven his wife to imbecility, and is as inexorably and stonily religious as ever. Next David visits his aunt's house at Dover. She lives in her old home with Mr Dick and Peggotty.

Commentary

There is David's reaction to change before the comic exchange with the waiters over Traddles. There is both a depressing and changeless focus in the Inn, but the reunion with Traddles is fine compensation. Traddles's capacity for games shows a refreshing lightness of character (that is not a derogatory term) and Sophy is a gem in terms of organizing capacity and arrangements. Traddles's account of his marriage negotiations carries a comic verve, and David's appraisal of that marriage is of an ideal partnership. Mr Chillip's account of the Murdstones is a terrible duplication of experience with a strong emphasis on the hypocritical religiosity of Murdstone's attitudes. The next moving reunion for David is with his aunt, Mr Dick and Peggotty, Betsey being made very angry by the thought of 'that murdering woman of a sister'.

insalubrity unhealthiness.
Gray's Inn one of the inns of court which has the privilege of calling candidates to the bar.
Westminster Hall A famous court of law, used here by Traddles as a symbol for his chambers.
cockboat cockleshell.
Britannia-metal A cheap substitute for silver.
DOE *dem* A legal practice in the courts, used before the reform of common law procedure in 1852.
pounce powder used to dry ink.
wafers thin pieces of dried paste used for sealing letters.
the Sultan's famous family The Sultan Haroun-al Raschid in *The Arabian Nights*.
negus sweet wine, water and sugar, served hot.
recovered the conduct i.e. got over the behaviour of Betsey on the night that David was born.

Chapter 60

David discusses with Betsey the question of whether Agnes has any attachment. Betsey tells him that she suspects Agnes has. David goes to Canterbury to visit Agnes, and finds that Mr Wickfield is much restored in health. Agnes is now running a small school. David determines that he will try to change the brother-and-sister relationship between himself and Agnes.

Commentary

There is a delightful focus on the happiness of the emigrants and David is brought up to date with their doings and other news by Betsey. David is apprehensive about Agnes, and realizes that Betsey is criticizing him somewhat for having stayed away from Agnes for so long. We also note Betsey's cunning in not being specific about Agnes's attachment – in a way she is teasing David, who is obviously (to us) the attachment. His reunion with Agnes is an emotional one. Agnes wordlessly reveals her devotion to David by keeping everything as it was when they were children. There is a touching if somewhat sentimental scene between father and daughter. David continues to call her 'sister', thus inadvertently putting some distance between them.

every stone was a boy's book An effective way of stressing David's intimate associations with the place.

Chapter 61

David goes back to London, and continues a witness to the happy married life of Traddles and Sophy. He visits a model prison at the invitation of his old schoolmaster Mr Creakle, now a Middlesex magistrate. Traddles, who bears no grudges towards Mr Creakle, goes with him. They find that the two prisoners who are exhibited as models are Littimer and Uriah Heep. They are as hypocritical (and successful) as ever because they are able to take advantage of the system, which makes converts and penitents.

Commentary

More autobiographical associations with Dickens's own writing career and aspirations open this chapter. Sophy shows how practical and helpful she can be (we are reminded of the contrast with Dora) and Traddles shows how good-naturedly and deservedly happy he is. Their pleasures are simple but real. The visit to the prison shows (a)

Dickens rounding off part of his novel and (b) waxing satirical about the over-comfortable treatment of prisoners, even in their isolation. There is a telling comparison made with the world outside. And in fact the words of Littimer and Heep stress that they have not changed, merely conformed to what they know is required, just as they did in life. The ironic and rather black humour shows David aware of the fact that he is being blamed for what has happened to these two men. The best moment of this chapter is in the account of Miss Mowcher's determined capture of Littimer.

jobbed illegal work.
Tower of Babel See Genesis, 11,4–9.
the neophytes i.e. those being initiated.
as if they had just come into church A brilliantly economical way of showing how hypocrisy – here Littimer's – is treated with a kind of reverence.
Immaculates i.e. free from stain – a continuation of the religious imagery.

Chapter 62

Betsey continues to push her suspicion that Agnes has an attachment, and David goes to Canterbury to ask Agnes to share her secret with him. It becomes apparent from her manner that she is far from being averse to David, and he tells her that he loves her. He finds that she is in love with him and that she has been all her life. They go to Dover to tell Betsey the good news. They are married within a fortnight, and Agnes reveals to David what Dora said to her on her deathbed.

Commentary

David is constantly drawn to Agnes, as we see from his visits, and his own deep love for her becomes more and more apparent to him. Betsey is deliberately teasing and forecasting at the same time. David's questioning of Agnes shows him as an emotional blunderer, and shows us that side of Dickens which is incurably romantic. The revelation to Betsey shows just how much that good soul has despaired of David's ever getting things right with Agnes: she has hysterics. Dora's final bequest of David to Agnes carries the terrible irony of what might have been had David known his mind, and his heart, sooner.

Chapter 63

We are ten years on, and Mr Peggotty comes back from Australia to visit David and Agnes. His news is uniformly good. Mr Micawber is now a magistrate and a most respected member of society at Port Middlebay; the one-time usher 'Dr' Mell is there too. David accompanies Mr Peggotty to visit Ham's grave at Yarmouth before he returns to Australia. A tuft of grass and some earth from the grave are taken in response to Emily's request.

Commentary

A picture of family bliss is followed by Mr Peggotty's appearance. His news is of Emily's sacrifices on behalf of others, her repentance being carried through in this practical morality; he also explains her timidity. He tells how Mrs Gummidge rejected marriage and how loyal she has been to him. The newspaper report of Micawber's activities (and the temporary reappearance of 'Dr' Mell) is a piece of fine satirical-comic humour, and Mr Micawber's own effusions to David, now a famous author, are typical of the man we have come to know and love.

the singing of Non Nobis *Non Nobis Domine*, a canon often sung instead of 'Grace After Meat'. It was composed by William Byrd (1538–1623).
Terpsichore the Greek goddess of dancing.
Sol the sun.
Though seas between ... roared An adapted quotation from one of Mr Micawber's favourites, 'Auld Lang Syne'.
your Eagle course i.e. soaring upwards to greater successes.
remote ... unfriended ... melancholy ... slow A deliberate echo of the opening line of Oliver Goldsmith's *The Traveller* – 'Remote, unfriended, melancholy, slow' (1764).

Chapter 64
Summary and Commentary

This is a rounding off of everything, particularly in relation to the main characters of the novel. It takes David into full marital happiness and Betsey into old age, accompanied by the ever-faithful Peggotty. The latter still retains the Crocodile-Book. Mr Dick flies his kites, Rosa and Mrs Steerforth continue to quarrel. Julia Mills becomes rich, Traddles even happier. The novel closes with a paragraph of praise, almost religious, about Agnes.

Revision questions on Chapters 49–64

1 Write an account of the storm at Yarmouth and its effects.

2 Compare and contrast the characters of Rosa Dartle and Mrs Steerforth from these chapters.

3 Write an essay on the most dramatic scene in these chapters.

4 How far are you convinced by David's ignorance of Agnes's feelings for him? Refer closely to the text.

5 'Rounding everything off spoils the novel.' Discuss.

6 Write an essay on either (a) the emigrants or (b) the visit to the prison.

Dickens's art in *David Copperfield*
The Characters

There are nearly one hundred characters mentioned or examined in *David Copperfield*, and it would be impossible in the space given here to treat them all. Below you will find selective analyses of the most important. Dickens is equally adept at drawing men or women, while his best characters are undoubtedly his oddities and grotesques. He has a tendency to draw characters who are either black or white in terms of their moral attitudes – Heep is unquestionably evil, while Traddles is white throughout. But it would be a mistake to apply this judgement too rigorously, for Dickens can shade characters as well, and perhaps a close look at Mr Micawber (who is feckless and blinkered as well as endearing) will confirm this.

I think it is true to say that all the characters have a marvellous fictional reality of their own, drawn from the vividness of Dickens's conception of them and the essentially dramatic presentation. Dress and physical appearance, particularly the first impact, are often the prelude to the real investigation of character; think of Micawber, Miss Mowcher, Steerforth, Miss Murdstone. The characters' names are often suggestive of their nature – Betsey Trotwood is quick to say that naive Mrs Copperfield married a *murderer*.

Other aspects that rivet the reader's attention include the application of a character tag – thus Mr Micawber is always expecting that 'something will turn up'. Another is a physical action, like the writhing of Uriah Heep. Remember that it is part of the narrative art of Dickens that all the characters in *David Copperfield* are seen through David's eyes, since he is the first-person narrator of the action. But all characters exist in terms of human relationships, and obviously the problems of courtship and marriage stand very high in the personal interactions of this novel. The range is from boyish calf-love through romantic courtship to seduction, while the marriages presented are both happy and unhappy. Annie's remark, which David takes home to himself so strongly in Chapter 45, perhaps reflects Dickens's appraisal of his own state – 'There can be no disparity in marriage like unsuitability of mind and purpose'.

David Copperfield

Persevering, self-reliant, self-denying.

David is a superb character: sharp, observant, sensitive; as a child in need of warmth and love, as an adult capable of additional effort and commitment to safeguard his position. He is also, like most of us, capable of human error: he is so impressionable and susceptible that he is given to exaggerated worship or infatuation. We have to suspend rational thought once we enter the narrative, for David is shown to have a superhuman power of recall. Once we have got over that, we recognize the psychological consistency with which David is presented.

The early chapters show David as adult looking back on David as child. We note immediately the quality of his observation, seen in the first chapter with the vivid depiction of Betsey Trotwood. There is also some telling observation of Mr Chillip and, almost in passing but very important to our assessment of David later, a notation of his mother's weakness. This is carried into the second chapter and beyond; we note that David is both inquisitive and insecure: asking Peggotty about marriage, fearing the presence of Murdstone and having intuitive feelings about that gentleman. We also note that the direct warmth and love in his life is supplied by Peggotty. Murdstone and his friends recognize David's imaginative capacity and perhaps fear his deductions when they call him 'Brooks of Sheffield'. Despite this, and the child's wondering uncertainty, we note that David only *suspects*, and that he does not understand. It is here that we first come to a positive appraisal of Dickens's art; he is so identified with the child David that he is able to convey all the tremulous naivety and innocence that make his suffering to come all the harder to bear. Despite this, his accuracy of recall establishes his mother's vanity, the egoistic core which is going to lead to her own emotional imprisonment. It is a tribute to Dickens's acute insight that David, who loses his mother, is to grow up and marry a spoilt, impractical and doll-like girl who resembles her at every turn. The loss is overcome, but with debilitating consequences.

David has a child's interest in the experiences of Yarmouth; again we are aware that he is responding to the *warmth* of family life. He is, as he puts it, sensible of Mr Peggotty's goodness. His capacity for wonder and his natural interest (these are to serve him well as a writer) are shown in his appraisal of Mrs Gummidge. His interaction with Emily further underlines his own innocence; but from time to time we are aware of the man looking back at the boy, and imposing the man's judgement – the might-have-been if Emily had not grown up and been seduced by David's best friend. The contrast between home and Yarmouth provides a brief lyrical interlude in David's life before home shows him the prison-house of the emotions. But Yarmouth provides a telling interlude, and such is David's loyalty and his emotional associations with his friends there that he returns to them as his family in the later years of his success.

David craves kindness, and receives none from the Murdstones. The lessons, the punishments, the fears, the reduction of his mother which he watches daily, all these are David's lot, his compensations being found in Peggotty and the retreat into the rich world of books. David's early life is an example of adversity providing future material. Even here David shows his spirit, his biting of Mr Murdstone being but scant repayment of that gentleman's sadistic religiosity. Before he is sent away there is a moving exchange with Peggotty, through the keyhole, which stresses David's isolation and the warmth he feels for her family.

His journey with Barkis again displays his ignorance, but also indicates his capacity to respond to people and his delight in their company. If his sensitivity is exposed by the greedy waiter, it is further injured – David is nothing if not vulnerable – by his having to wear the placard when he gets to Salem House. Even here his insight is tinged with compassion, and we feel that the visit to Mr Mell's mother shows his latent humanity. His first sufferings are once more those of isolation, since he is there in the holidays. With the arrival of the boys he experiences some torment but, more importantly, he meets Steerforth and is taken over by that handsome, imposing, selfish, condescending and hero-worshipped character. Steerforth is a genteel bully who rarely needs to display anything more than an indolent charm. Steerforth's self-confidence gives David the security he has craved, though – and this is where his insight is revealed – David sees certain flaws that are later to become important, as in Steerforth's disgraceful treatment of Mr Mell. His reading to Steerforth shows the intensity of his emotional need; it also helps prepare him for his future profession as a writer of fiction.

I have stressed David's emotional needs. There is no better example than his reactions when he returns home and finds that he has a baby brother. His mother kneels and puts his head next to the baby's: David writes:

I wish I had died. I wish I had died then, with that feeling in my heart! I should have been more fit for Heaven than I ever have been since! (Chapter 8)

David spends a last happy day with his mother and Peggotty before the return of the Murdstones in the evening. The next day David is humiliated by them, and also has to see his mother humiliated too when she compares the baby's eyes to his. His birthday–deathday is indeed a memorable one. He has to endure (no criticism of Peggotty) the account of his mother's life with the Murdstones by his old nurse; then comes the next humiliation, which is work in the warehouse. Before that David makes an important judgement after the funeral:

The mother who lay in the grave, was the mother of my infancy; the little creature in her arms, was myself, as I had once been, hushed for ever on her bosom. (Chapter 9)

This kind of sentimental association never leaves David; it leads, perhaps indirectly, to Dora.

After Peggotty's marriage David becomes 'at ten years old, a little labouring hind in the service of Murdstone and Grinby'. These are traumatic times for him. It must be admitted that it shows a certain snobbery in him, but it also brings him friendship with the Micawbers, friendship of dubious financial value but of very positive warmth.

David's determination to escape from his degrading employment shows his spirit, his courage, his need for greater self-expression and fulfilment. In part his determination is speeded by the departure of the Micawbers, who have been an emotional prop to his existence. But once he moves we are aware of his extreme vulnerability – David when young is born to be put upon, witness the affair of the box, the terror of the slop-shops and the terrifying encounter with the sadistic and violent tinker. But Betsey Trotwood, the searched-for aunt, becomes effectively a surrogate mother. David finds his first real security with her and with Mr Dick; kindness is what he needs, and it is also what he responds to. The putting down of the Murdstones by Betsey plus her joint guardianship of David (now Trotwood to some) with Mr Dick gives him practical hope, the feeling that he now can do justice to himself. Because of his aunt he is transformed overnight from vagabond in his own eyes to respectability.

David's sensitivity is further brought out in his response to Agnes and, perhaps more positively at this stage, to Uriah Heep. At Dr Strong's he keeps his eyes and ears open (he is early suspicious of Jack Maldon), and is also somewhat moved by Mr Wickfield's signs of distress. David now becomes raconteur par excellence, his descriptions, particularly of the Old Soldier, showing his talent and his future vocation. His arrival in London shows him eager for experience (hence the theatre visits) but unsophisticated, and the timely re-meeting with Steerforth begins his man-about-town education, though not in any dissipated sense. David, ever open to influence, takes in the effect of Mrs Steerforth, Rosa Dartle and, quite decisively, the impact once more of Steerforth himself. He registers the cold and unruffled efficiency of Littimer. But always his own feelings of nostalgia come through; he returns to Yarmouth, to Mr Omer and his friends, even bursting into tears such is his susceptibility when he sees Peggotty. But his hindsight as narrator makes him aware that Steerforth is playing a game, particularly in relation to Little Emily.

David is easily taken out of himself, marvelling at the diversion and grotesque personality of Miss Mowcher. He treasures his own affection for Emily – it is sentimental – and is seriously put out by her concern for Martha and the latter's situation. Fortunately in one sense, David is faced with a career decision about whether he should be a proctor or not. He is as ever appreciative of Betsey's efforts on his behalf. David's interview with Mr Spenlow shows him in humorous vein, something he is to indulge satirically as he comes to know the practices of the Commons more intimately. This humour, and an attendant impracticality, is also displayed when he finds himself elevated into 'chambers' by his aunt's goodness. There is something naive about the way David begins to *live* now – the boy has become the man almost overnight. That first dinner-party and the presence of Steerforth (followed by the unfortunate meeting with Agnes) shows him, albeit unsteadily, in a man's world. It is a chastening experience. There now begins the interaction with Agnes which leads David to consider her as his Good Angel, but as a sister only. David also is initiated into society, and treats it with some irony. How close Agnes is to his heart is shown in his reception of Heep's ambitions with regard to her – he is filled with disgust, distaste, a kind of unease, also a kind of resentful passion.

David visits Mrs Steerforth and Rosa Dartle in the company of his returned friend, and then takes leave of him for the last time in friendship. Though suspicious and a little uneasy, David is straightforward enough in his own dealings to have no inkling of what Steerforth is up to. David's visit to Yarmouth is initially to see the dying Barkis; he shows that he has mastered the fundamentals of his career when he sorts out Peggotty's legal affairs after her husband's death. But he is overcome by Emily's departure and Steerforth's betrayal and concerned for his own unwitting part in this terrible situation. This moves him to supportive action, and he accompanies Mr Peggotty to the abortive interview with Mrs Steerforth. After this, David returns to his romantic obsession with Dora. It is a blind and besotted period of his life, as he courts the girl who appears to have been made in his own dead mother's image.

David's concern for others is shown in his attempts to protect Traddles from getting into debt on Mr Micawber's account, but he is soon involved in crisis himself when Betsey announces that she has lost all her money. It is a tribute to David's natural warmth that he is more worried on Mr Dick's account than his own, and that the generous ideal of living for others is certainly present within him. In a brilliant excursion into his own consciousness David examines his fears about being poor; they are all on Dora's account. When he tries to disentangle himself from Spenlow and Jorkins he fails; he also experiences further unease when he speaks to Agnes and realizes that what he most fears, the net of Uriah Heep, is tightening around her.

David's main function now is that of narrator and observer of (a) the section that involves Dr Strong, the Old Soldier, Mrs Strong and Jack Maldon and (b) the further decline of Mr Wickfield. More important still is his amazement when he learns that Mr Micawber is to work as Heep's confidential clerk. He has also to adjust to his new situation of greatly reduced means. He tries to inspire Dora with his own practicality, but to no avail. He meanwhile undertakes shorthand in order to report the Parliamentary debates, endures being found out as Dora's suitor by Miss Murdstone, further endures Spenlow's rejection of him, and then has to face the crisis of Spenlow's sudden death. In reaction he recurs to Julia Mills's diary, which reflects his confidences, hopes and sentimental effusions to his now out-of-reach Dora. He also visits Canterbury and becomes uneasy about the state of Mr Micawber's mind.

David has to show considerable character during this visit to Canterbury, since there is the scene involving Wickfield's outburst against his own degradation in front of Heep. His return to London finds him in continuing crisis, for Mr Peggotty has his report of Emily. The courtship of Dora through her chaperones has its moments of humour, and David has his continuing blanket blindness to the limitations of his beloved. The marriage day is narrated in a kind of repetitive nostalgic rhetoric, but soon David has to cope with the disasters of housekeeping; it is a tribute to his tolerance, self-discipline and continuing hard work. He is also very grateful for Betsey's tenderness towards Dora, which sustains him during this early period of his marriage. David has in fact a marvellous resilience; he also has a tremendous capacity for hard work, seen in his writing, yet there is some pathos in his contemplation of his 'child-wife' in the evenings.

David finds himself caught up in the Dr Strong business before it is resolved through the agency of Mr Dick. Out of it comes an important recognition, for Annie's words register with him strongly – 'There can be no disparity in marriage like unsuitability of mind and purpose' – 'no disparity in marriage like unsuitability of mind and purpose' (p. 654), the repetition showing the weight of the cross that David has to bear. He is also oppressed by Littimer's revelations about Steerforth's abandoning of Emily, by the incident with Martha, by the surfacing of Betsey's supposedly dead husband.

At the back of all this is success. His book is published to acclaim. It is compensation for his anxiety on a number of levels. He is also able finally to take himself away from 'the music of the parliamentary bagpipes'. There follows a quarrel with Dora, which greatly upsets him and which demonstrates how powerless he is against the tenacity of her childlike character. He abandons the idea of forming her mind, is oppressed by the shadows of the future, but happy that his friends are proud of his growing reputation as a writer. The real oppression is the physical weakness and illness of Dora; he feels the inevitability, though he does not voice it, of her coming death.

Again there is a compensatory focus for David to attend to, and this is Micawber's denunciation of Heep, which removes one of David's major worries and, in simple plot terms, rescues Agnes. The finding of Emily is further source for David's concern. Events now hasten towards their conclusion. Dora dies, David has what seems to be a breakdown, and goes abroad. Before this there is the departure of the Micawbers and the deaths of Ham and Steerforth. David's life is always punctuated with incident. He is greatly disturbed before these deaths in the chapter called 'Tempest' which seems to underline (a) the disruption of his own life by grief and (b) the disruption of other lives close to him. He does his duty by Mrs Steerforth and Rosa, unprepared for the terrible bitterness Steerforth's death arouses in the latter. David takes his suffering abroad.

There he devotes himself to his writing and his absence occupies three years. We may consider this a long time, but David's reaction is an extreme one. He believes, misguidedly as it turns out, that Agnes is out of his reach. When he does return he fails to take Betsey's hints about the state of her heart, but eventually comes to his fulfilment with her.

David has some nobility of character, a capacity for dedication, loyalty in friendship, considerable imaginative talent and a genuine kindness and concern for others. We are perhaps somewhat amazed by his blindness over Dora, but it is the blindness of infatuation to which we are all subject from time to time. Above all, David rings true from beginning to end, and it is no accident that the largely autobiographical element in his portrayal makes for psychological authenticity and integration. The tracings from boyhood to adulthood are convincingly done. He is essentially likeable, his primary interest, like that of his creator, being in people.

Mr Micawber

A thoroughly good-natured man, and as active a creature about everything but his own affairs as ever existed.

In any study of *David Copperfield* Mr Micawber must take pride of place. He is one of Dickens's greatest comic creations, though he is attended from time to time throughout the narrative by a degree of pathos, generally because of his inability to keep afloat economically or, much later, because he is liable to be arrested at the suit of Uriah Heep. In Chapter 11 we are given an account of his physical appearance as he appears at Murdstone and Grinby's, when he presents himself as landlord to David. He is middle-aged, stoutish and bald, wears shabby clothes but has an impressive shirt-collar. He also has eccentricities: he carries a cane and has recourse to a quizzing-glass. He has great difficulty in surviving financially, is constantly being dunned by creditors and is now used to being shunned by Mrs Micawber's relations. He is pompous to the point of magniloquence, coins a number of impressive phrases, always has words at his command and, even in dire adversity, will give a dinner, mix punch, sing and recite before the inevitable threat of suicide. Mr Micawber has a kind of dignity and is a born survivor; debtors' prison and pawnshop are alike grist to his histrionic mill. His maxim still applies today: 'if a man had twenty pounds a year for his income, and spent nineteen pounds nineteen shillings and sixpence, he would be happy, but that if he spent twenty pounds one he would be miserable' (pp. 165–6). He is a great qualifier of what he has said, usually employing the words 'in short' before saying simply what he has already uttered with sublime verbosity. His language is embellished by literary and biblical reference; sometimes accurate, sometimes adapted. Shakespeare and Robert Burns are his favourites.

As we have seen, Micawber alternates between moods of extreme cheerfulness and optimism – 'something will turn up' – and the complete depression of spirits in which he feels himself beset by terrible adversity and terrifies Mrs Micawber by dark hints as to the possible use to which he may put his shaving materials. Sometimes his transitions of mood, of hopes and fears, are so sudden that he can begin a letter describing himself as 'a drifting wretch whose doom is sealed' and reopen it before posting to add a postscript describing himself and his family as 'at the height of earthly bliss'. Micawber is naturally convivial, and this is what makes his mood in the shadow of Heep so untypical and of course so worrying to Mrs Micawber.

He is a natural family man, and that family increases, a living testimony to the warmth of love subsisting between himself and his wife. The latter has the greatest confidence in his abilities, always intent upon high office for him in his chosen career, almost before he has begun it. Micawber is active in all affairs except his own, but his is an important moral function at the heart of the novel: his talents, his sense of right and wrong, cause him to employ himself in finding out the deeply nefarious nature of Heep's crimes. These he exposes with fitting and typical emphasis through repetition, taking delight in writing the letter that begins the revelations (he is an inveterate letter-writer) that lead to the downfall of 'HEEP'. Good, warm, irresponsible but with a moral core and a core of humanity, Micawber finds himself in his exposure of Heep. For in choosing to betray the confidences he has obtained as Heep's confidential clerk, he chooses a way of life that is a promise of much greater future security. He demonstrates that what appears is not what is; a man who provides comic/pathetic interludes in the life of David, he becomes practical, penetrating and organized. The details are left vague, but it is consistent that the man who bluffed his creditors should prove himself capable of bluffing Heep, who finally exposes himself. He merits success after this in Australia, and reports of this success are couched in the familiar Micawber style.

Mrs Micawber

I never will desert Mr Micawber!

A fecund woman whose family is ever increasing, Mrs Micawber has the one outstanding quality of loyalty, though she is hard-pressed to maintain it when Mr Micawber becomes moody as he chooses to conceal from her what he has discovered about Heep. She resembles her husband in many ways and has abundant faith (or affects to have) in his abilities. She is always considering courses of action he might take. She is just as roundabout in expression as he is. And just as her husband can be alternately flung down by events and rise triumphantly above them, so too can Mrs Micawber surface to be the life and soul of a social gathering after a fainting fit from extreme depression of spirits. She is an optimist and she is, like him, convivial, so that she can enter into the spirit of the social occasions that help to make their lives bearable. She has been forced to accept, one deduces, a somewhat lower standard of existence with Mr Micawber than she enjoyed at home. But she has her own particular humorous idiosyncrasies, such as when we learn that she studied the marriage service the night before she married Mr Micawber and came to the irrevocable conclusion that she never could desert him. It is an endearing interpretation of the 'for better, for worse, for richer, for poorer', the last phrase being the operative one as far as she is practically concerned. She is not only optimistic, she is convinced of Mr Micawber's talents and feels that any pecuniary sufferings they are forced to endure spring from the world's lack of appreciation of Mr Micawber's great qualities. She even blames her own family for their blindness to her husband's abilities. She represents loquacious wifehood, chaotically delighting in her children and confident that her husband will win through to success, which he does.

Uriah Heep

this detestable cant of false humility

If the Micawbers represent the pathetic/comic in social existence, then Uriah Heep represents positive evil, the kind of evil that wears down goodness by sheer cunning and the ability to turn any situation to advantage. David first meets him when he stays at the Wickfields'; Heep has a cadaverous face and is about fifteen years old at the time. His 'long, lank, skeleton hand' particularly takes David's attention. In fact David is fascinated, in a repugnant way, by Heep, who is quick to ingratiate himself. He points out early on to David that he is studying law with a view to advancing himself. He always refers to himself as 'a very umble person', but this masks a rooted and determined personality, with a considerable resentment of those above him. In David's case, though Uriah cultivates his company, this comes to mean a jealous obsession over David's interest in Agnes, which is in conflict with Heep's own. That wish – to get Agnes for himself – partakes more of the Beauty and the Beast analogy than of reality.

At one stage (in Chapter 39) Uriah gives an account of his own and his parents' education in charity schools (which does as much to explain him psychologically as Steerforth's home life explains his arrogance and the fact that he will not brook being crossed). Heep snarls in adversity but never sheds his 'umbleness', as his final appearance in gaol in Chapter 61 shows. There is innate evil in his makeup, and his subterranean malignity is frightening.

Heep calculates, and only in the case of Micawber does he calculate wrongly. His cover is fawning hypocrisy, but as he advances so the accretions of power emphasize his waspish quality. We see his ambition and his ruthlessness in his gradual undermining of Mr Wickfield, but the best-laid plans of monsters and men can fail if they are not too scrupulous in their checking up on employees. Heep here 'bites the hand that fed him', and he adopts those bad companions of fraud and forgery to achieve his ends – complete power, both financial and emotional.

In the process of ruining Wickfield financially he also drives him to the point of madness because of his desire, crude lust, for Agnes. Heep's malignity seems to be almost a reflex of his personality, so that he virtually insists on being the instrument to confront Dr Strong with his wife Annie's supposed loveless feelings for him. Strictly, this is none of Heep's business but his rise is accompanied by seemingly motiveless revenge on the society that has seen him in his early mock humility. Mr Micawber's exposure of Heep shows the latter's Achilles' heel – with all his cunning and cleverness he is unable to stop Micawber. If Heep has one redeeming feature it is his affection for his mother, and she is the only person to show any affection for him. Yet in his adversity she cannot reason with him. Heep is grotesque, his red hair and his gestures a filling-out of the character. The physical characteristics suggest the mental ones, and as we study Heep in action we realize that this provides a deepening which goes beyond the mere outline caricature. The damp fish-like hands rubbed together suggest the coldness of his nature. He is so vividly drawn that his physical repulsiveness almost comes off the page at the reader.

Betsey Trotwood

An eccentric and somewhat masculine lady with a strong understanding.

Strictly, Betsey is David's great-aunt, and her first appearance in the story is an unpropitious one, since she leaves David's mother when she finds that her child is a boy and not the girl she had forecast and would doubtless have treasured. We learn that Betsey married a man younger than herself who treated her brutally – he once tried to throw her out of the window – and that she separated herself from him, thereafter living as a single woman under her maiden name. Although it is believed that her husband has died he proves to be very much alive, providing a mystery in the plot right up until his funeral (such as it is), which is attended by David and Betsey. There is no doubt that she has been blackmailed into giving him money. Betsey was initially soured, so much so that in her newly-found determined 'spinsterhood' she virtually conditions her maidservants into staying unmarried. Human nature being what it is, they usually fall in love and reject her advice. As we come to know Betsey, so we come to love her the more fully; she develops from caricature into character, becoming more rounded, less sour, more sentimental though still practical, less severe and stern. The outward Betsey is 'tall, hard-featured' and has a certain 'inflexibility in her face, in her voice, in her gait and carriage'. Initially David finds all this fearsome, as does the reader; but beneath this disciplined and contrived exterior Betsey shows herself from time to time to be soft and caring in a very positive way. When David goes to Dover he finds her aggressively defensive over the donkeys, but he also finds that she cares for his physical needs with practical kindness.

Betsey has a bark and a bite, showing the latter when she has to put down that mordant duo, the Murdstones. We feel that here she is activated by straight insight into their particular brand of righteous evil. Doubtless her behaviour too is coloured by her memory of that defenceless 'child', David's mother, so easily put upon, so easily reduced. Betsey is fearless and to a point domineering; but if we look closely at her protection of Mr Dick and her undoubted if gruffly expressed affection for him, we realize that she is kind to the core and has the courage to cock a snook at opinion and value the simple man who would be thought mad (and perhaps treated as such) by so many. In effect, she becomes a surrogate mother to David, providing for him generously at school and in his career, and being the first to impose little sacrifices on herself when she fears that she has lost all her money. These may be white lies, but they cover a generous soul who is trying to shield Mr Wickfield. Later she is to extend her generosity to Mr Micawber in his emigration.

Betsey is a wise woman, witness her treatment of Mr Dick outlined above. She has her suspicions about David's love for Dora and particular doubts about Dora's nature. When David asks her to give Dora the practical benefit of her advice she refuses to do so, knowing that there is no way a third person can step equably between husband and wife. In fact her wisdom extends to appraisal of character, and she almost senses that David was bound to choose someone in the likeness of his mother. Her own psychological integration is consistent, and her confiding in David ultimately about her husband shows her sensitivity and her need for love. She is in some ways enlightened, as she shows when she tells David 'Never . . . be mean in anything; never be false; never be cruel' (p. 224), and she has a particular quality of courage that enables her to face both financial and emotional adversity. There must, however, be a tendency among readers to remember her for her eccentricities, which add spice to her character and comic interludes in the plot. She is fiercely determined that the donkeys shall be kept off her green; she consults Mr Dick before undertaking any course of action and elevates his pronouncements to a level of unarguable wisdom. Her speech is full of her prejudices (like her attack on the 'pagan' name of Peggotty). Her investing David with the name 'Trotwood' is a consciously loving identification.

As David's career at school and Doctors' Commons progresses, so Betsey becomes softer in temper (and in effect) and there is an increase in her reflex generosity and kindliness. She treats Dora with something more than tolerance – probably a warmth that she has acquired, taken to herself, because of her love for David. One other thing remains – Betsey's uprightness of character is complemented by her uprightness of figure. Even in her old age she walks through the winter weather with the indestructible verve she has always displayed.

Mr Dick

The most amenable and friendly creature in existence.

Mr Dick reflects his creator's enlightenment over the treatment of mental illness and Betsey Trotwood's enlightenment in her treatment of him. He has been virtually looked after by Betsey for ten years when we first meet him. His brother has had him placed in a private asylum, but Betsey takes him over and invests him with a human dignity and particularity that is profoundly moving. Mr Dick is simple but harmless, kind, helpful, given to good offices on behalf of others (witness Dr Strong) and has a gentle nature. His obsession is with the account of his affairs for the 'Lord Chancellor, or the Lord Somebody or other'. Out of this memorial he strives to keep out any reference to King Charles's head, for he believes (Betsey calls this an allegorical mode of expression) that some of the trouble that was taken out of King Charles's head was put into Mr Dick's. What is quite remarkable is Betsey's faith in him (whether deliberately assumed for his sake or genuine we shall never know). He lives a sheltered existence, rambling in his mind – and with his kite – and rattling his money. His vacancy is complemented by a general cheerfulness, but he is grateful to Betsey. His naivety, his essential innocence, make him a winning character, and we note that at Canterbury he is not teased by the boys but becomes popular because of his obvious good nature and his capacity to make toys and trifles. He is very fond of David and he becomes warmly attached to Dr Strong, seeming to provide that learned and kindly man with sympathetic support.

Mr Dick has a functional role in the plot. In Betsey Trotwood's financial adversity he does copying work of some value. But more important than that is his bringing into the open Mrs Strong's love for her husband and her devotion to him. Here he fulfils all Betsey's faith in him and, though we may find this somewhat unrealistic, in the context of the sequence Mr Dick fits, since we are dealing with the symbolic innuendo of good and evil, typified by Dr Strong and Annie on the one hand and the shadowy Jack Maldon and the virulent Heep on the other. It can be argued that to define his actual role in the revelations and reconciliation is difficult since his part in it is so vague. So is Mr Dick, but his general goodness has the effect of bringing out the goodness of others.

Steerforth

his handsome face turned up, and his head reclining easily on his arm. He was a person of great power in my eyes.

It is a great tribute to Dickens's powers of characterization that Steerforth does not degenerate into a stereotype. He is not merely the head boy of Salem House; he is on terms of more than equality with members of staff (witness his treatment of Mr Mell), deferred to, privileged, knows himself to be superior and has a kind of natural arrogance and condescension, which comes from being spoiled. There is no one in the school of sufficient stature either physically or morally to stand up to him. He gets his own way, indulges himself (note the way he takes David over with regard to the nightly ritual of reading) and has a lordly manner that is meant to convey breeding but which in fact conveys an egoistic sensibility that makes use of others. This is achieved in two ways by Steerforth: he either pretends that people don't exist, or he exerts his automatic charm to propitiate them in his favour. He never fails: he has wealth and natural gifts and a proud and over-indulgent mother; the result is that he inherits her qualities and has them magnified because of her weakness. He extends his patronage wherever he goes, and we are aware of his conscious snobbery; there is also in him a contained sadism, though this appears to have been unleashed against Rosa Dartle in his youth, and certainly there is verbal sadism as well as snobbery in his attack on Mr Mell. We see him of course through David's eyes, and David's own insecurity is lessened by the friendly condescension that Steerforth shows him. Steerforth is indolent, and he picks up, if he feels like so doing, whatever chance puts in his way. Thus when he meets David in London it provides an excuse for the mild excess of drinking; more serious is his opportunistic attitude, concealed under charm and friendship, when he meets the essentially simple people of Yarmouth. He quickly dismisses in his own mind the 'chuckle-headed' ignorance (and innocence) of Ham; Emily is his prey, and though the seduction is distanced and somewhat melodramatic – hardly one of the realistic strands of the novel – we find Steerforth despicable. David has mixed feelings, disliking his old patron but at the same time being fascinated by him and admiring some of his qualities.

Steerforth is presented with an admirable consistency. His youth at Salem House foreshadows the kind of man he will become, indeed, already is. He takes over David's pocket money and spends it for him, gets special consideration from Mr Creakle, whom he tolerates splendidly, and is a thorough snob (witness Mr Mell). We have pointed out that he uses David, but one of his questions to his young admirer – 'You haven't got a sister, have you?' – gives sufficient indication of his interest in seduction. As long as his mother keeps him supplied with funds, seemingly for ever, Steerforth has no intention of entering on a career. All his abilities, when they are stirred from indolence, serve his own selfish ends.

Steerforth may be contrasted with Uriah Heep, since their physical disimilarities only serve to emphasize what they have in common –

the need for power, the gratification of their desires, and their contempt for those whom they use and abuse. Steerforth is adept at the casual sneer, observing that David's Yarmouth friends are 'the natives in their aboriginal condition'. There is no doubt that his choice of Littimer is a deliberate one, for Littimer, without his master's advantages, is a mirror-image of his coldness and selfishness. Steerforth's disgraceful treatment of Emily is compounded when he tries to pass her on to Littimer, who has observed his treatment of her and would doubtless behave towards her in the same way. Only once does Steerforth show some consciousness of his own moral defects, and that is in a brief but telling exchange with David in Chapter 22, p. 319. He even shifts the blame here to the way he has been brought up. True, but the excuse cannot stand examination. Steerforth is regarded by many critics as a stereotype, but I feel that he is given an admirable if distanced consistency. If he is not a fully rounded character it is because he lacks the overall moral fullness to become so. And occasionally we meet that kind of incompleteness in life.

Traddles

He was very honourable, Traddles was

David first meets Traddles at Salem House, where he is often to be seen 'in a tight sky-blue suit that made his arms and legs like German sausages, or roly-poly puddings'. Consequently he is a butt for others and can be made miserable, though he is by nature cheerful. To adapt Wordsworth's phrase, the boy is father of the man. Because he is good-natured and patient he is a ready-made victim for such a sadist as Creakle (though notice that Traddles bears him no ill-will in later life); and just as at school he is imposed on, so in later life we find him putting his name to one of Mr Micawber's bills and taking his wife's sisters into his own home. He is uncomplaining generally, and gets down to the hard work of reading for the Bar with his customary good nature, tolerance and spirit of endurance. After all this he gets what we hoped he would – he becomes a successful barrister, more than useful in spelling out the legal position with regard to both Heep and the ever-pursued Mr Micawber.

One of his boyish qualities is the habit of drawing skeletons, this providing for him a kind of refuge from his troubles – a practice he carries into the law courts when he has moments of idleness. Whatever he does, his 'comic head of hair' will not be smoothed down, and this gives him an eccentric appearance, what Dickens calls a permanently 'surprised look'. Traddles contrasts at every turn with the evil characters in *David Copperfield* – he is the epitome of goodness. Strangely this is not cloying, for he gives to others without thought of anything but their need. He contrasts with David in his choice of a wife; he endures, with fortitude but with an endearing loyalty, his absence from his fiancée when he is working very hard. Traddles does not know what temptation is. His greatest happiness, though he probably does not realize it, is in serving others. Nor is he without courage. He is the only boy who dares to reprove Steerforth for his treatment of Mr Mell. He is a good friend to both David and the Micawbers, making their interests his. Sophy is his treasure, and he has a kind of nobility in his acceptance of her family; such is his degree of tolerance that he doesn't appear to regard this as a burden.

Of all his fine qualities perhaps his modesty best stamps him for the natural unspoiled soul that he is. He describes himself as 'a plodding kind of fellow' and 'not a bad compiler' but with 'no invention at all – not a particle'. Yet he proves to have a down-to-earth practical flair, knowledge and command of situation when he deals with Heep after Mr Micawber's explosion. Nor should we underestimate his ability. He becomes a judge, having made the most of himself without any egoistic emphasis of ambition, and made the most of others by his unselfish devotion to them.

Dora

She had the most delightful little voice, the gayest little laugh, the pleasantest and most fascinating little ways.

The diminutives in the above description are Dickens's ironic way of emphasizing the 'child' quality in Dora, which David finds so endearing and which is domestically debilitating. Her similarity to David's mother must be stressed, for this is part of the subtlety of Dickens's presentation. She is spoiled and does not live in a real world; when that real world intrudes, and she experiences it she finds, like the Lady of Shalott, that it is too much for her, and she goes into a decline and dies. She is at first protected by Miss Murdstone, while her imagination, what there is of it, is supplemented by the experiences, real and simulated, of Julia Mills. She is playing at life, her caresses lavished upon Jip while her other protector, her father, dies and gives way to the maiden aunts. These soon allow David his limited visits, and the courtship prospers in a conventional way.

Dora cannot endure any pressure. Conflict or argument is beyond her limitations, while domestic practicality is a foreign language, which David tries to teach her without success. Before marriage experience deepens her a little, everything about Dora is on the surface – her appearance, her curls, her manner, her timid innocence, her playfulness, her trust, her singing and painting. Her father in his lifetime affects to rule but in effect she rules him; David's nervous excitement evokes a like response in her, with the exception that his is real whereas hers is too much for her. David realizes that she is regarded as a precious toy, secluded from life. This is the be-all and end-all of her position and David's destiny.

David knows in his heart that Dora is childish and irresponsible, but deliberately turns two blind eyes towards what he knows he sees. When he tells her of his new poverty she responds by saying that 'I'll make Jip bite you', and then begs him not to be practical, 'because it frightens me so'. Betsey sees into and through this small and transparent plant, appropriately christening her 'Little Blossom'. Housekeeping is almost a dirty word to Dora (the oyster incident is perhaps the funniest). David brings reason to bear but without success. She is hopeless but comes to know that she is hopeless. She asks 'Doady' to think of her as his 'child-wife'. Doady has already become practical in other directions in order to sustain their marriage, and though there is no hint of any major split between them we feel that his necessary other activities help to keep him balanced. There *is* an attendant pathos about Dora, for we sense that she realizes she has failed her intelligent, sensitive and hard-working husband. But David should not have expected anything else from her. Her decline arouses compassion in the reader; her self-knowledge coming at the last is poignant. She sends for Agnes on her death-bed, and expresses the wish that she and David will come together when she is gone. There is something mawkish about this, by today's standards, but indeed Dora seldom enters the real world. She is an exaggerated character, but with enough of truth to be a disturbing one too. Common sense requires an effort that she is constitutionally incapable of making. The loss is David's, but he remains kind and loving to the end.

Agnes

A quiet, good, calm spirit

If Dora is hardly of this world, then Agnes is infinitely too good for it. She has all the virtues that Dora lacks but, though we are aware of her calm, her wisdom, her sincerity, her essential goodness, the tranquillity she always inspires in David, we are also aware that she has no sexuality, no positive personality traits that register with the reader. Worse still, she has no faults. The result is an amalgam of goodness rather than a character drawn from life; she is too self-sacrificing to be true, too staid and not vital enough to elicit any response from the reader. She is a 'better angel', sister, guide and support to David; she is a little woman in relation to her father even when she is a child, and she undergoes no development as a person. She is stable, worthy, kind and dull, and, what is hardly surprising, David takes a long time to come to the knowledge of his love for her. She has an insight into the essential evil of Steerforth, and warns David against him after she has seen David drunk at the theatre with his friends. Although she says to him at the end, 'I have loved you all my life' we wonder exactly what kind of feeling she is describing. She has displayed a patience and restraint above normal powers, particularly when David confides to her his love for Dora. Here she is calm, understanding, disciplined; she is rational – we might be inclined to say too rational – in advising him to write to the Misses Spenlow. No waves of repression ripple the surface of her responses in her perfect attitude to Dora after she and David are married. She is in fact so much a controlled friend that David can hardly believe that she loves him in the normal way. The lack of passion, based supposedly on uncertainty of his reception, is seen in the length of time that David stays away. Her goodness makes the happy ending of the novel a descent from realism into the world of sentiment.

Other Characters

David Copperfield is a richly peopled novel, and it is possible for readers to investigate any of the characters in some depth, although a few are merely stereotypes. *Peggotty*, in fact, plays a major part early in the novel because of her care for David, her loyalty to him and to her mistress, her dislike of the Murdstones as well as her distrust of them, and the fine comedy of her courtship by Barkis and, sadly, his being incapacitated and dying. Her later life is somewhat in the shadow of her brother's worry over Emily and his determination to bring her home. She is devoted to David, and is very easily moved (as he is) for she bursts into tears of happiness whenever they are reunited. It is she who tells David of his mother's last days; she is impulsive, brave (remember how she gets to David and tells him that he is to be sent away to school) and generous (she wishes to lend David money). She helps him with his house in London. A measure of her generosity of feeling is shown by the fact that – though David suffers agonies for having introduced Steerforth to his innocent and trusting Yarmouth friends – Peggotty never reproaches him about it. It would be true to say, I think, that in her eyes David can do no wrong.

There is a fullish description of Peggotty in Chapter 2; she has very dark eyes, and 'cheeks and arms so hard and red that I wondered the birds didn't peck her in preference to apples'. She is very plump too, so that whenever she exerts herself greatly – whether in affection or anger – 'the buttons on the back of her gown flew off'. She is usually busy and is a capable housewife, which, after all, is what Barkis really wanted. In their relationship there is a good deal of burlesque. Peggotty's loyalty is almost stretched to unreality – after the death of David's mother she finds herself 'willing' (like Barkis) provided that David is not against her marrying. David isn't, and she acquires a house of her own, a horse and cart in which to visit David at Blunderstone and the sentimental possibility of being buried one day 'not far off from my darling girl'.

Barkis himself is caricature. Initially presented with humour – note the long pauses in his speech when he is with David – his use of David as go-between through the enigmatic phrase (to the boy) that 'Barkis is willing' and the later nearness, as well as the comedy of the marriage, all this is Dickens writing with verve and delight in the creature he has created. But somehow Barkis's death and the flight of Emily strike the sombre note that has the reality of life and, more particularly, the changes life brings. Dickens maintains a splendid perspective in characterization.

Mr Peggotty has recognizable family similarities with Peggotty. He is kind, has sacrificed much on behalf of others and takes a great and unselfish joy in it. If his devotion to Emily and Ham and his actions are understandable, then his taking over of Mrs Gummidge can only be seen as a remarkable demonstration of altruism, particularly in view of her misery, which is at first undoubtedly natural but, after that, self-indulgent. There is repayment in the long term, for after Emily's flight and Mr Peggotty's anguish on her account Mrs Gummidge becomes progressively more and more unselfish and appreciative of the position in life that Mr Peggotty has made for her. None the less it must be observed that Mr Peggotty, Emily and Ham each exist as symbols, the first evocative of all that is good, loyal and long-suffering.

Ham may be 'chuckleheaded' by Steerforth's definition (and perhaps the reader's too) but he is impressive physically, and innocently simple in his devotion to Emily. More than that, he is brave ('When theer's hard duty to be done with danger in it, he steps for'ard afore all his mates'). His character is geared to the sacrifice of his life on behalf (ironically too late) of the man who has already wrecked his life by the seduction of Emily.

Emily hardly exists as a character. Those early idyllic childhood days with David, in which there is a superabundance of sentiment and singularly little positive colour or animation, give way to a young womanhood in which she is the cynosure of all eyes (and not a little gossip) because of her beauty and her wish to be a lady. Her engagement to Ham is unlikely and doomed; her ironic saving of Martha leads to one of the most melodramatic sequences in the novel, in which Martha in return saves her. Her exchange with the vitriolic Rosa shows her lacking in spirit. Emily is a stereotype, the fallen woman who is supposedly good and whose natural goodness means that she can be successfully reclaimed. In a plot of sentiment and melodrama, yes; in a context of realism, no. There is no substance to her character at all; she is brown paper rather than cardboard.

The Murdstones are recognizable caricatures. As a pair they are formidable when they are dealing with the weak (Mrs Copperfield), inadequate when they are dealing with the strong (Betsey). There is a mercenary consistency in Mr Murdstone's preying on weak young women and then, with the aid (sometimes) of his sister, reducing them so that they are completely under his will or, worse still, die. Miss Murdstone is cruel and uncaring, her treatment of David's mother and of David, plus her taking over of everything in the house (witness the keys) symbolizing the name and nature of power. Her role in relation to Dora is a degrading one; she is the official watchdog (Jip being merely a toy) and a spy, discovering David's letters to Dora and reporting them to Mr Spenlow.

Other cruel or unsympathetic characters are *Mr Creakle*, the tyrant of Salem House aided and abetted by his watchdog and voice, *Tungay*. There is a marked sadism in his treatment of the boys, particularly Traddles, and some cynicism in Dickens's registering of his rise in life, admittedly in retirement, so that he ends up as a Middlesex magistrate. He has softened with the years but is as blind to justice as he always was, and the visit to the prison shows that Mr Creakle has acquired only the inability to see the truth. *Jack Maldon* is outline caricature-selfishness only, his departure for the East focusing on the sub-plot of his supposed affair with Annie Strong, thought to derive naturally from their childhood friendship, to which the insensitive Mrs Markleham is constantly referring. He is too indolent for words (literally) and never for a moment comes alive even figuratively or emotionally. Of far greater substance, though still in the area of caricature, is the repugnant and self-seeking, cold and infinitely calculating *Littimer*. He appears initially to be the respectable gentleman's gentleman, but this is a mask for, we suspect, a like corruption to Steerforth's own. His willingness to take on Emily, to accept his master's cast-off mistress, is surely indicative of the low moral level on which he exists. His recounting of his travelling life with Steerforth and Emily, his opportunistic attempts to cash in on what he knows and to make immediate capital as and when he can, show the degraded nature of the man.

The other male characters vary in liveliness, though it must be acknowledged that their life is that of puppets rather than people and they are used, to continue the image, to pull the strings of the plot. *Mr Mell* stands in contrast to Steerforth. The poor usher, by his situation of 'respectability' in a school, cannot of course acknowledge the existence of his mother in an alms-house. But Mell himself is quite kind to David, and his spirit and quiet dignity in response to the arrogance of Steerforth makes an effective social and moral comment, which Dickens is careful to stress. With his rise – like Mr Micawber's – in Australia, we see that Dickens is establishing a kind of consistency, for Mell has too much spirit and ability to be wasted in the degraded atmosphere of Salem House. *Mr Omer* is a delightful character, his asthma and joviality and functional commentary marking David's comings and goings over the years. He is a genuine Dickensian eccentric.

Mr Wickfield is rather different, subdued and oppressive, his weakness not fully explained; his dependence on Agnes gives way to his dependence on Heep, his one outburst marking the anguish of the man. He has a capacity for concealment that shows his inner suffering. *Dr Strong* complements Mr Dick. He belongs to that unreal strand of the plot that sees goodness undermined by rumour, observation and innuendo, not least from his garrulous mother-in-law. He is an enlightened and cultivated man, the situation with his young wife an intriguing one, but Dickens does not explore that relationship at any depth. It is maudlin and sentimental – and melodramatic – and Dr Strong emerges, like Mr Peggotty, as the epitome of goodness. His marriage is that of cardboard father to cardboard daughter; there is altogether too much unanimated acceptance on his part, and too much kneeling-at-his-feet on hers, for us to see the relationship as anything but morally, domestically symbolic. *Mr Spenlow* is sparsely drawn, his acceptance of David, and his putting down of him when he learns of his love for Dora, almost subsumed in the suddenness of his death and the abject state in which he has left his affairs. *Mr Jorkins* is more powerful in reference than in person. Rather than living up to his irascible and authoritarian reputation, he slopes away from responsibility with some speed. *Mr Chillip* is in at the beginning and near the end, another genuine eccentric who is initially overcome by the sheer power of Betsey's manner.

We have considered Emily in passing, but we should give some attention to *Mrs Copperfield*, largely because of what I have suggested earlier – the fact that Dora's personality touches certain chords in David that bring back his mother. We get the impression that she is weak, vain, easily flattered, as we know from her asking David what was said about her by Mr Murdstone and his companions on the day when they took David out. We know that she is a hopeless housekeeper, and that she relies heavily on Peggotty. We know too that Betsey considers her a mere baby, but we remember too that despite her insubstantiality she and David and Peggotty have some happy times together before Peggotty marries Barkis. Her last goodbye to David is moving in the extreme, almost as if she senses the future, while the scene between her, the baby and David is poignant in view of that future.

Mrs Gummidge has again been referred to, and she is a fine piece of caricature. Strangely, as we have seen, she develops, the goodness she receives rubbing off on her. The transformation of the 'lone lorn creature' is not, however, convincing. *Annie*, Dr Strong's wife, never comes alive, but her mother *Mrs Markleham* certainly does. She is called the Old Soldier because of her ability to organize 'relations against the Doctor'. She does more than that; she organizes her daughter's innocent past with Jack Maldon against him, and is largely responsible (together with the malevolent Heep) for the rumours that attend a happy marriage. She is always in good voice and, though caricature, is expressive of danger to her daughter's marriage.

Mrs Steerforth is the imperious mother of James; cast in an inflexible and arrogant mould, she is proud, snobbish, domineering, reduced by a terrible stroke when she learns of her son's fate. Before that she has been reduced by Rosa too, for the latter holds her responsible for Steerforth's death and, quite succinctly, for Steerforth's life of self-indulgence. *Rosa Dartle* is a miniature study in abnormal psychology (compare her with Miss Wade in *Little Dorrit*) with the scar not merely physical but a permanent wound in her personality. Her savage scenes, with both Mrs Steerforth and, terribly, with Emily show the venom that lurks in her personality. She knows she is Steerforth's dupe, and her companion role with Mrs Steerforth is a form of imprisonment. Yet, in a curious and embittered way, Rosa likes the prison.

Martha Endell is pure melodrama. She is the fallen woman who seeks to save Emily from her kind of life; she nearly takes her own life, and goes to Australia, where she prospers and marries. She represents the evils of prostitution (Dickens of course never mentions the word) but there is no real sinful life – or any other life – in her. *Miss Mills* enjoys her role of confidante, go-between and adviser in affairs of the heart, her own having once been wronged, while the *Misses Spenlow* keep up the formality of courtship on Dora's behalf after her father's death. *Mrs Crupp* is the idle landlady whom David has the misfortune to have in his chambers. Everything is too much trouble for her, but Miss Betsey is much too much for her, and puts her down. Of all these minor characters *Miss Mowcher* is outstanding in terms of speech, personality, size – a vivid and idiosyncratic beauty specialist who knows evil when she sees it and has the courage and will-power to deal with it. There is nothing more direct in the whole of *David Copperfield* than her citizen's arrest of Littimer:

He cut her face right open, and pounded her in the most brutal manner, when she took him; but she never loosed her hold till he was locked up. She held tight to him, in fact, that the officers were obliged to take 'em both together. (Chapter 61)

Always the Dickensian touch with character has its own vividness.

Style

David Copperfield employs the first-person narrative, which conveys with immediacy the experiences of life; we must never forget, however, that we are reading a work of fiction, and that the autobiographical tone is an assumed one (we could think back to Defoe's use of the technique in *Moll Flanders*). Autobiographical connection between Dickens's life and *David Copperfield* will be found elsewhere in this commentary, but here we are concerned with narrative art and the various stylistic modes employed by the author. The first-person narrator is looking back, selecting incidents from his childhood and young manhood that seem to have been formative, and which contain the substance of his developing life. Most of these are referred to in the character-sketch of David that heads the section on Dickens's narrative art. *Retrospect* is therefore the major narrative device of this novel. Within this there is a variety of mood, much of it sombre (the Murdstones), much of it humorous/pathetic (the Micawbers), some of it lyrical (David in reaction to his love for Dora), some of it sentimental (Peggotty, Dr and Mrs Strong), and some of it plain melodramatic (the Rosa Dartle and Martha Endell episodes). The main areas of stylistic concern in *David Copperfield* are given below.

Dialogue

Throughout his life Dickens had a great and practical interest in drama, putting on private theatricals and even on occasions touring and reading from his works. This may well account for the excellence of the dialogue in his novels; in *David Copperfield* there is a very high proportion in the narrative. Most of it is in what we would call 'received standard English', the main departure from this being the Yarmouth sequences, where the dialect of Mr Peggotty and Ham, for example, is conveyed with naturalness and ease. Dickens was the master of the kind of speech that establishes idiosyncracies of character, as in Mr Micawber or Uriah Heep. By the same criteria Betsey Trotwood, Mr Dick and Steerforth come alive, though their registers are essentially different. David in retrospect and in interaction with others speaks in a standard register, and it must be allowed that it is quite unrealistic that Martha and Dr Strong should use precisely the same kind of language, despite the fact that he is an expert on words – a mid-19th-century Dr Johnson – while she is a prostitute. This lack of differentiation in speech means that some sections of the novel are more aurally realistic than others. But Dickens has a wonderful ear for natural speech and speech rhythms – take the scenes at Salem House; David's first dinner party; the idiom of Mrs Crupp; David discussing his aunt's loss with her. Or – and this is where Dickens is particularly effective – note how Dora's speech is *her*: her little childish affectations, whether baby-dog-talk or baby-husband-talk to Doady. The range is remarkable, and Dickens's control of dialogue is one of the marks of his inimitability – he is a verbal ventriloquist, who enters into the *speech* of the characters and caricatures that he describes.

Description

Any novelist depends for his effects on description – of people, scenes, exteriors and interiors – and Dickens is a wonderfully stimulating observer of both persons and things, with an outstanding and unusual eye for detail. I say unusual because Dickens stresses the grotesque or the individual trait to such an extent that it seems to take over the character – like Mr Micawber's tortuous verbosity; Mr Dick's kite; Uriah Heep's writhing; Rosa Dartle's scar, which appears to be alive. Always there is this emphasis on the *visual*. Physical appearance, even dress, is described, often on the first appearance of the character, but this is a Victorian convention to which Dickens subscribed. Shall we ever forget the first descriptions of Betsey Trotwood, the Murdstones, Mr Micawber or Uriah Heep? Their appearance, gestures, mannerisms, are imprinted on our consciousness. It is so too with such interiors as the boat at Yarmouth, where the miniature nature is given a considered stress, and contrasts with its inhabitants' largeness of heart. Consider David's dwelling, always in detail, on churchgoing with the Murdstones in Chapter 4, or the sketch of mental, emotional and physical dilapidation that constitutes the schoolroom in Salem House. Interiors are a Dickens speciality, and when the crowded emigrant ship sets sail we are below deck with the emigrants in their new quarters which will take them to a new life (Chapter 57). The outstanding piece of exterior description in the novel is the storm and its build-up at Yarmouth in Chapter 55. Here the force is *symbolic*, for its fury and its destruction (the threatening and fateful atmosphere is cunningly suggested) is prophetic. By this I mean that it stands for the destructive elements in the novel, notably Steerforth, whom it destroys. The storm takes with it Ham, who has already been destroyed by Steerforth's seduction of Emily, destroyed within though as courageous as ever without. This is *irony*, for it is a comment on the life of the one and the death of the other. One other description of note among the many also has a symbolic force, and this is where David and Mr Peggotty follow Martha in Chapter 47, when she is about to attempt suicide. The effect is nightmarish, surrealistic, a social and moral commentary on degradation, suffering and poverty, which breed diseased bodies and diseased minds:

> Slimy gaps and causeways, winding among old wooden piles, with a sickly substance clinging to the latter, like green hair, and the rags of last year's handbills offering rewards for drowned men fluttering above high-water mark, led down through the ooze and slush to the ebb-tide. There was a story that one of the pits dug for the dead in the time of the Great Plague was hereabout; and a blighting influence seemed to have proceeded from it over the whole place. (Chapter 47, p. 671.)

This is another symbol, and needs to be studied carefully for its full effect to be estimated. As so often with Dickens, the state of buildings and scenes in their disintegration are a form of comment on the state of individuals and society. Here the scene is the state of Martha and the kind of society that has made her. The significance of the selected detail – such words as slimy, sickly, green hair, rags, ooze, slush, plus the reference to the Great Plague are Dickens's way of indicating moral and social contamination. His style is always vivid with particularity.

Pathos

Dickens is a sentimental writer, and *David Copperfield* has its share of sentimental scenes and situations, though for the most part he manages to avoid the self-indulgence of the great death scenes of his earlier fiction, notably those of Little Nell in *The Old Curiosity Shop* and of Paul in *Dombey and Son*. The death of David's mother and her baby, for example, or of Barkis, are treated with quiet and becoming dignity and reticence. Consequently there is an increase in genuine pathos, for instance David being confined to his room at home, his loneliness at Salem House wearing his placard and, in his full maturity, his travelling after Dora's death before he comes back into life with Agnes. There is pathos too in Dora's realization of her failure as a wife and her desire that after her death David should marry Agnes. There is the pathos of Agnes's contemplation of her father's drinking degradation and its results as he goes into 'partnership' with Heep. There is the pathos of Traddles at Salem House; the pathos of Betsey in relation to her husband, and the running pathos of David's marriage to Dora. But again the spread is uneven. The reader should be moved by the contemplation of the love – and suspicion – attending the marriage of Dr Strong and Annie, but here the artificiality of the prescription is too obvious. Chief recipient and provider of pathos is Mr Peggotty. Again the feeling is that this is too sentimentally coloured, as indeed are the scenes involving Emily as well as her letters.

Humour

We have already indicated some of the main facets of Dickens's humour, but although *David Copperfield* is in some ways a sombre book, there is much humour, notably that stemming from the verbal eccentricities, both spoken and written, of Mr Micawber, as well as situation humour involving both Micawber parents, Mr Dick, Traddles, Miss Mowcher, Betsey and Mr Chillip. The Misses Spenlow's eccentricities add more, and even the miniature of the waiter who systematically robs the small David of his food and drink exists in a comic element. Dickens is skilful in devising situations that bring out to the utmost the well-defined eccentricities of his characters. The celebrated interview at Dover between Betsey and the Murdstones – with the donkey background – is full of rich denunciations of the Murdstones' way of life. Effective here is Betsey's ignoring of Miss Murdstone. Another denunciation scene involves Mr Micawber's repetitive and rhetorical condemnation of Heep, though here the humour has to be shared with the dramatic intensity.

Miss Mowcher's scene with Steerforth and David is redolent of wit and verbal humour; the contemplation of Mrs Gummidge before her later reform has the comedy of self-pity; Barkis's questioning of David with regard to Peggotty is comedy that partakes of limited communication and silence. Sometimes there is an inevitability about the humour – like Peggotty's buttons shooting all over the place, or Mr Spenlow's invoking Jorkins as monster whenever there is a situation he cannot handle. Mrs Micawber's refrain line that she will never desert Mr Micawber is perhaps over-used, but we should note that it is completely within character. Part of the humour consists of a running irony, often of a prophetic nature. A good example of this occurs in Chapter 21, where Steerforth observes that 'the sea roars' as if 'it were hungry for us'. Ham says that he would lay down his life (for Emily) 'most content and cheerful!' Steerforth 'told a story of a dismal shipwreck . . . as if he saw it all before him', while Emily kept away from Ham. This is a grim ironic look into the future of all three of them – a kind of dark comedy.

Satire and Social Comment

Much of Dickens's work, from *Oliver Twist* onwards, contains a studied and effective exposure of social evils, and *David Copperfield* has a wide range of reference, the moral propagandist in Dickens never allowing his narrative to take second place to his indictment of social abuses. *David Copperfield* is in some ways a carry-over from *Nicholas Nickleby* in its emphasis on education, though the farm schools of Yorkshire and the particular evils of Wackford Squeers have given place to a southern equivalent in Salem House and the malevolent Mr Creakle. He is brutal and ignorant, terrorizing by constant flogging, a worthy recipient (from the Murdstones' point of view) of David, whom they have tried to rule by the rod. It is obvious that this is what Dickens considers a school ought not to be, though when he presents us with Dr Strong's we are perhaps amazed by the vagueness; here there is plenty of liberty and recreation, and it is described as the 'best' school, and as 'different from Mr Creakle's as good is from evil'. This appears to be an idealization by Dickens free of satirical intention – a kind of benign influence ruling, conditioning and preparing the children for life. Uriah Heep's charity school is described in Chapter 39 of the novel. Here a false sense of servility is apparently taught, and this produces the fawning hypocrisy of Heep, seen as he crawls his way up, and later in his model-prisoner behaviour. Dickens's ideas were based on those of the great educational reformer Friedrich Froebel (1782–1852), the German who believed that the faculties were best developed by a child's voluntary and pleasant activity, without any sense of coercion. Dickens himself wrote an article on Froebel's kindergarten system in his magazine *Household Words* in 1855, some seven years after *David Copperfield* began to come out in monthly numbers.

Dickens had personal experience of the effects of imprisonment for debt, witness his father's incarceration and Dickens's derivative fictional treatment of this in *Little Dorrit* (1855–7). There is some drawing of the squalid life in the King's Bench prison in *David Copperfield*, Micawber being a regular victim or near-victim; a man could be arrested at the instance of creditors and flung into one of these prisons if he could not pay his debts. Often conditions were of the utmost squalor, but those prisoners who had money (often because they did not choose to pay their debts) could buy in anything they wanted. By an Act of 1813 prisoners could petition for their freedom, but often the gaolers were corrupt and the Act could not take full effect. Eventually imprisonment for debt was abolished by the Debtors' Act of 1869, except for those people who had had judgment given against them but still refused to pay their debts.

The main satirical shafts against the law come from Dickens via David. Doctors' Commons bears the weight of the major ridicule. This fellowship of lawyers, called advocates and proctors, had the exclusive rights of appearing in all Ecclesiastical (which at that time included divorce), Admiralty and Probate cases. The business of Doctors' Commons was dissolved in 1857, its concerns being dealt with by separate courts and its members being merged with ordinary barristers. Dickens directs his satire at the fact that the same set of people were frequently to be found dealing with diverse cases; that the same men were sometimes judges and sometimes advocates; that there was too much time and expense given to trivial cases; that it was all a kind of game which paid the lawyers well and cost the litigants dearly. Perhaps the most positive satire occurs in Chapter 39, where there are people touting outside Doctors' Commons for marriage licences or the proving of a will. The law, witness Mr Spenlow, was dominated by snobbery, and barristers were divided from solicitors (then called attorneys).

But if this is satirical, there is some bitterness in the conditions hinted at in the private asylums and the treatment of the insane in the period. In Chapter 14 Betsey tells David the story of Mr Dick, and of how, sent by his relatives to a private asylum, he had been ill-treated, hence she had asked him to stay with her. The power of the relations here and the ignorant treatment is offset by the natural goodness of Betsey. Next prisons get the Dickensian treatment, and here there is a definite edge of satire. This stands in contrast to Dickens's other views, for we see the conservative within the radical in his responses. As a result of the influence of the great prison reformers John Howard and Elizabeth Fry, one or two prisons had been built in which prisoners were kept in separate cells without the possibility of contact with one another. Dickens had visited such a prison in Philadelphia in 1842, and in his *American Notes* (published in the same year), he considered this separation as being a cruel and unnatural method of treating prisoners. It was misguided and worse than bodily torture. But in England a prison modelled on these lines had been built at Pentonville, with the idea that local authorities in their turn could set up similar establishments; there were fifty of these in England by the time Dickens came to write *David Copperfield*. Dickens attacks the system by showing that the separated model prisoners have fooled the authorities, not been conditioned by them, that just as they acted out roles in life, so they have adapted those roles to prison existence with consummate success. They are thought to have become good, and to have been made so by the system. They have in fact remained bad, and the system has given them the opportunity to indulge in evil.

General questions

1 In what ways is *David Copperfield* a novel that invokes a vivid picture of childhood?

Guide-line notes:

(a) introduction – a clear indication of those chapters in the novel that deal specifically with childhood. (b) David's earliest memories – his mother and Peggotty as influences. (c) the happiness at home with them in the pre-Murdstone era. (d) the holiday in Yarmouth – calf-love and Emily. (e) the return from Yarmouth. (f) mother's remarriage. (g) David's sufferings. (h) David's compensations (reading, Peggotty). (j) punishment(s). (k) away to school. (l) account of school (some detail, reactions, Steerforth, Traddles, Creakle etc. (m) visit from Mr Peggotty/Ham. (n) summoned home after mother's death (earlier note needed on birth of baby brother). (o) funeral – Peggotty's narrative. (p) the wine-bottle task (q) the Micawbers and incidents. (r) running away – incidents. (s) treatment by Aunt Betsey. (t) putting down of the Murdstones. (u) at Dr Strong's – selected incidents. (v) Conclusion – vivid evocation through retrospect – child's view of adults – skill of treatment since it is an adult telling the story – vividness of memory – establishing of standards etc.

2 Write an essay in appreciation of the autobiographical method of narration. In what ways is it an advantage to tell the story in this way?
3 Write an essay on the use of coincidence in *David Copperfield*.
4 What do we learn of life in early 19th-century England from this novel? Refer closely to the text in your answer.
5 By reference to specific examples, illustrate the use made by Dickens of (a) physical descriptions and (b) particular phrases.
6 Select any two or three incidents from the novel in order to illustrate Dickens's dramatic or humorous use of dialogue, or both.
7 Discuss the development of David's character. In what ways do you find him interesting?
8 Compare and contrast Uriah Heep and Mr Micawber.
9 Indicate the influence upon David of (a) Mr Murdstone, (b) Mr Creakle and (c) Peggotty.

10 Write an account of the character of Betsey Trotwood, bringing out clearly her main qualities.

11 Compare and contrast Steerforth and Littimer.

12 'Too good to be true.' How far would you agree with this statement on the presentation of Mr Peggotty, Ham and Emily?

13 Compare and contrast Dora and Agnes, saying which you prefer and why.

14 With reference to any two incidents, write an essay on Dickens's ability to create atmosphere in *David Copperfield*.

15 Which scenes in the novel do you find most melodramatic and why?

16 Indicate the part played in the novel by (a) Traddles, (b) Mr Dick and (c) the Spenlow aunts.

17 Indicate in what ways *David Copperfield* is a novel that embodies social and moral comment in its narrative.

18 What do you learn of Dickens's views on education from any particular incidents in the novel?

19 Which do you think is the funniest scene in the novel and why?

20 Write an essay on any aspect of the novel not covered by the questions above.

Further Reading

Charles Dickens: A Critical Introduction, K. J. Fielding (Longman)

The Dickens Theatre, Robert Garis (Oxford University Press)

The Moral Art of Dickens, Barbara Hardy (Athlone Press)

Who's Who in Dickens, John Greaves (Elm Tree Books)

Dickens and Women, Michael Slater (Dent)

Dickens and Charity, Norris Pope (Macmillan)

Dickens and the Invisible World, Harry Stone (Macmillan)

The above is merely a selection from the mass, but the first book provides a most sensible and balanced introduction to Dickens. For the student who is completely won over to him there is the opportunity to join the Dickens Fellowship and receive copies of *The Dickensian*, a magazine devoted to the writer.